Winter along the Trace. The Natchez Trace in the wintertime presents a picture of serenity and beauty. In contrast to this modern-day image were the hazards of travel which once plagued the early wayfarer. Snow and intense cold in the winter, overbearing heat and humidity in the summer, and biting insects—not to mention the highwaymen and outlaws who frequented the environs, ever ready to rob and kill unsuspecting victims—were just a few of the constant dangers which lurked along the old Trace.

THE NATCHEZ TRACE
A Pictorial History

James A. Crutchfield

Rutledge Hill Press
Nashville, Tennessee

The official emblem of the Natchez Trace Parkway is a silhouette of a post rider on horseback. The old Trace, during a great portion of its later use by Americans, served as a post road connecting Nashville and Natchez. As such, it was a vital communication link between the lower Mississippi valley and the settlements in the East.

ISBN: 0-934395-03-9

Published in Nashville, Tennessee, by Rutledge Hill Press, Inc., 513 Third Avenue South, Nashville, Tennessee 37210.

Typography by ProtoType Graphics, Inc., Nashville, Tennessee

Library of Congress Cataloging in Publication Data

Crutchfield, James Andrew, 1938–
    The Natchez Trace: a pictorial history.

    Bibliography: p.
    Includes index.
    1. Natchez Trace—History. 2. Natchez Trace Parkway—Description and travel—Views. 3. Indians of North America—Natchez Trace—Antiquities.
4. Natchez Trace—Antiquities. I. Title.
F217.N37C78   1985   976.2   85–11774

Printed in the United States of America
4 5 6 7 8 9 10 — 96 95 94 93 92 91 90

Dedicated to all of the men and women
who have traveled the Natchez Trace—
from time immemorial to the present

Parkway Headquarters. The Visitor Center at Tupelo, Mississippi, serves as the administrative headquarters for the Natchez Trace Parkway. Exhibits, an orientation film, a sorghum-making demonstration in the autumn, and a nature trail all contribute to a better understanding of the old Natchez Trace and the trials and tribulations of its early travelers.

Foreword

The purpose of the Natchez Trace Parkway, as stated by Congress, is "To provide a recreational parkway from Nashville, Tennessee, to Natchez, Mississippi, following the Old Natchez Trace. This roadway, generally following the historic Trace for 450 miles, will ensure a continuously unfolding inspirational interpretation of an important transportation route and its related regional resources which opened the way to expansion of the United States into the Old Southwest. At the same time, it will link the many outdoor recreation and historic sites developed for the enjoyment of the parkway visitor."

The route of the Natchez Trace is truly a path of cultural and scenic delights. Few other places in this great nation offer such a variety of scenery, natural and human heritage, and the opportunity to identify with the struggle of our forebears to develop this great nation. Much of the beauty of the parkway is the variety of scenery that it provides as it passes through three quite different types of topography. This variety creates a continually changing scene for the traveler that contributes to the total experience and lack of monotony of the parkway.

Interpretation on the Natchez Trace Parkway emphasizes the historical as well as the contemporary experiences of the people living along the entire length of the parkway, introducing the visitor to the continually changing parade of lifestyles and crafts of this region. Using the interpretive theme "The Roots and Routes of Man," we tell the story of the development of the Southeast which parallels the development of the entire nation, emphasizing man's dependence upon the land.

Despite all that it offers, the Natchez Trace Parkway is one of the less known and publicized national parks. Visitors who discover the parkway by accident are impressed with its beauty and the wealth of history associated with it. Immediately they make plans to return when they can spend more time exploring and absorbing the multitude of activities and experiences.

Contributing to this lack of publicity is the absence of written material—few books are available about this unit of the National Park System. And what is available is out-of-date.

Fortunately, Mr. Crutchfield's book helps fill this void. Here for the first time is a contemporary, up-to-date account of the human and natural history of the Old Natchez Trace and modern parkway. Available at last is an accurate and authentic account of the entire span of 10,000 years of events, written in a popular, easy-to-read style. Mr. Crutchfield writes with empathy and understanding because he grew up in the Natchez Trace region.

One of the objectives from the Natchez Trace Parkway Statement for Management is "To foster public understanding and appreciation of the parkway's cultural values by memorializing and interpreting the historic Trace and the cultural events and people associated with it. . . ."

No publication meets this objective better than *The Natchez Trace: A Pictorial History*. Mr. Crutchfield captures in words and pictures the true feelings and mood of the natural and cultural heritage of the Natchez Trace. I recommend this book to everyone who wishes to learn more about the Natchez Trace Parkway and the rich heritage of the region through which it passes.

John S. Mohlhenrich
Former Chief Park Interpreter
Natchez Trace Parkway

Acknowledgments

There is no doubt that a historical writer's best friends are the books and other written materials that have already been compiled by other writers about his subject. Even though there is a noticeable shortage of published material available about the Natchez Trace, the above axiom held true for me also. I have listed the volumes that were of the most use to me in the bibliography.

In addition to extending gratitude to the writers of these previous books and articles, I would like to thank John Mohlhenrich, former Chief Park Interpreter at the Natchez Trace Parkway, and his staff for their assistance during my work on this book. John's co-operation in allowing me access to the hundreds of photographs in the Park Service's collection was a large factor in helping me determine the direction and focus of the subject matter of the book. Truly, without John's help, the present volume would be much less valuable than it is. Dale Smith, current Chief Park Interpreter at the Natchez Trace Parkway, has also been most helpful.

I would like to thank Les Leverett, *photographer extraordinaire*, who reproduced all of the photographs for the book. He worked many hours bringing aged, dim negatives to vivid life, and his keen sense of professional pride allowed only the best job possible to be done on each photograph.

Finally, I would like to say "Thanks" to my wife, Regena, who photographed most of the scenes that were not available in the Park Service's files. This was not our first collaboration, and each succeeding effort is more enjoyable than the last.

James A. Crutchfield
Franklin, Tennessee

Natchez, Mississippi. Natchez, the seat of Adams County, is situated on the bluffs high above the beautiful Mississippi River. The town was the capital of the Mississippi Territory from 1798 until 1802 and of the State of Mississippi from 1817 until 1821. With the advent of the steamboat, Natchez became one of the busiest cotton markets in the world, and even today it is a large shipping port for cotton, as well as for soybeans and beef cattle.

Photograph courtesy of the United States National Park Service

Nashville, Tennessee. In 1962, Nashville became one of the first major cities in the United States to adopt a metropolitan form of government. The seat of Davidson County, Nashville today is the accepted leader in the nation's music and recording industry. Situated at the convergence of three interstate highway systems—I-24, I-65, and I-40—Tennessee's capital is also prominent in the insurance, banking, and chemical industries and serves as an educational and religious center. Nashville's population of close to a half million makes it Tennessee's second largest city.

Photograph courtesy of William Jayne

Table of Contents

DAR Natchez Trace Monument. This stone monument, located at the southern terminus of the Natchez Trace in Natchez, was dedicated in 1909. It was the first of several such memorials marking the route of the old Trace which were placed throughout Mississippi by the Daughters of the American Revolution. The DAR was one of several organizations responsible for a growing public awareness of the historical significance of the Natchez Trace, and through its efforts a great deal of support was generated for the creation of the Natchez Trace Parkway.

Photograph courtesy of the United States National Park Service

Illustrations

Introduction

The Natchez Trace! To those of us who were raised in its proximity, the very name evokes visions of dark, shadowy forests infested with outlaws ever ready to pounce upon some innocent wayfarer. But cruising in air conditioned comfort down the Trace's successor, the modern Natchez Trace Parkway, one has very little sympathy or understanding of these dangers and other inconveniences and discomforts which afflicted the weary traveler of yesteryear. Torrential rains, biting insects, flooding rivers and streams, torrid heat, and bitter cold teamed together at times to make a journey along the old Trace nothing short of a totally miserable experience.

From time immemorial the foreboding trail saw the passage of wild animal herds migrating to the great salt licks around Nashville. Later, it witnessed Indians—both prehistoric and historic—plying domestic trade among their villages and towns in Tennessee, Alabama, and Mississippi. Then came a host of European and American travelers, ranging from explorers, traders, and soldiers to boatmen, frontier preachers, and highwaymen.

Only since the 1820s has the Natchez Trace been known by that name. Prior to then it was called the "Path to the Choctaw Nation" along its southern portion and the "Chickasaw Trace" throughout its northern course. When it became a widely used thoroughfare by the Tennessee and Kentucky boatmen on their return business trips from New Orleans through Natchez to Nashville and by the post riders for the delivery of the mail between Nashville and Natchez, it was officially called the "Road from Nashville in the State of Tennessee to the Grindstone Ford of the Bayou Pierre in the Mississippi Territory." It was only after all of its busiest activity had subsided that it picked up the name which has passed down to us through history.

In time, engineering improvements provided more convenient and practical ways to travel from place to place in the region serviced by the Natchez Trace. But the old road persisted over the years, and the United States National Park Service had the foresight to preserve this vital monument to the history of the Old Southwest by assuring that the new Parkway followed the original route as closely as was acceptable by good engineering practice. The modern-day traveler is provided with the sights and sounds—and in a small way, the feelings—of a bygone age.

Mount Locust Inn. Mount Locust, one of the most famous "stands" or inns along the Natchez Trace is shown as it appeared when the Natchez Trace Parkway was established in the late 1930s.

Photograph courtesy of the United States National Park Service

THE NATCHEZ TRACE
A Pictorial History

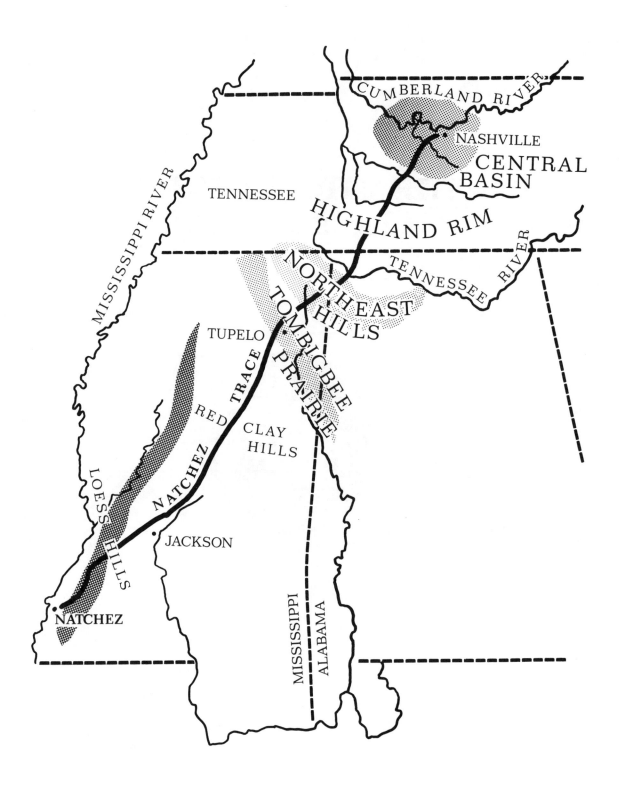

CHAPTER ONE

The Natural Setting

$\mathbf{A}$side from its modern paved surface, it is difficult to distinguish the Natchez Trace Parkway from its age old counterpart known as the Natchez Trace. While it was impossible during the Parkway's planning stages in the late 1930s and early 1940s to plot its path along the precise course of the old Trace, there is enough similarity between the routes of the two roads that whenever the Parkway is mentioned, one can also relate the conversation to the old Trace and vice-versa. In short, the two thoroughfares are synonymous, and when one speaks of one, he speaks of the other as well.

From its northern beginning just outside Nashville, Tennessee, the Natchez Trace travels in a generally southwestward direction. The northern end of the trail is located in the Central Basin of Middle Tennessee, with elevations averaging 500 to 600 feet above sea level. From there the Trace makes a slight ascent to the Highland Rim, and thereafter, for a few miles, attains the highest points—around 1000 feet—along its entire length. Leaving the Highland Rim in the southern part of Tennessee, the Trace descends into the Tennessee River valley of northern Alabama. From the point of its crossing of the river just west of Florence it climbs again, this time onto the Appala-

The Natchez Trace linked three of the largest watercourses in the United States. Beginning just south of the Cumberland River near Nashville, it crossed the Tennessee River in northern Alabama and terminated near the Mississippi River at Natchez. Altitudes varied along the Trace, but generally speaking, the road started out high in the north, around Nashville, and ended up low in the south, at Natchez. During its 450 mile journey, it traversed several distinct physiographic regions in Tennessee, Alabama, and Mississippi, as shown on the accompanying map. Today, Nashville is the most populous city along the Natchez Trace, with Jackson, Mississippi, next in size, followed by Tupelo and Natchez. Natchez is the oldest of the four, founded in 1716 as Fort Rosalie; Nashville is next, settled in 1779 and 1780; Jackson is third, established in the late 1700s as LeFleur's Bluff; and Tupelo is the youngest, incorporated in 1859, but dating its existence from the organization of the village of Harrisburg in 1832.
Drawing by James A. Crutchfield and Edison Travelstead

chian or Cumberland Plateau of Alabama and the neighboring Northeast Hills of Mississippi. These highlands, the western-most reach of the Appalachian Mountain chain, average from 700 to 1000 feet above sea level.

Crossing the Tombigbee River, the Trace enters Mississippi's Tombigbee Prairie. Elevations here drop to the 250 to 300 foot range. Entering the Red Clay Hills, the Trace climbs again to around 400 to 450 feet, but it is a short-lived ascent, and almost immediately it drops to the lower region around Jackson (about 300 feet above sea level). A gradual descent then brings the Natchez Trace to the Loess (pronounced LOW-ess) Hills of southwestern Mississippi and finally to its southern destination at Natchez. Elevations in this vicinity vary from 200 feet above sea level for the town on the Mississippi River bluffs, where the Trace actually terminates, to around 60 feet along the low-lying river. Absolute low and high elevation readings for the course of the Trace are 105 feet in Mississippi and 1,020 feet in Tennessee.

Since the changes in elevation along the Natchez Trace are minimal, altitude itself accounts for only subtle environmental variance. The Trace's 450-mile length, on the other hand, covering almost five degrees of latitude, does contribute to the existence of a diversity of ecological patterns. Because of the fairly great north-south difference—about the same as that separating Pittsburgh and Nashville—the Trace is divided into three distinct natural life zones.

On the northern end of the Trace from Nashville to Tupelo, the aboriginal countryside was once a vast mixed deciduous forest, consisting of oak, hickory, walnut, maple, and other species of hardwood trees. Today, much of this forest cover remains, albeit second growth, but it is interspersed with gently rolling cropland. This is typical hill farm country, and the wild-life which frequents its domain is represented by the white-tail deer, the bobcat, the raccoon, the grey and the red fox, the ever present opossum, the grey and the fox squirrel, the cottontail rabbit, a variety of hawks, the bobwhite quail, and numerous species of field and forest-loving songbirds.

The middle stretch of the Natchez Trace, lying in Mississippi between Tupelo and Jackson, was a mixed hardwood and pine forest in its early days. With settlement, however, most of the woods were cleared, and much of the land was converted to agricultural use. Cotton was the prevalent crop grown in this section, and it was the region's red clay soil which primarily supported the antebellum plantation system of farming. While the plantations are gone now, farming is still practiced heavily here, and the native species of wildlife include mammals and birds that have patterned their life styles around an agricultural economy: woodchucks, deer, bob-white quail, foxes, crows, rabbits, and a variety of cropland songbirds.

The Trace's southern section, from Jackson to Natchez, enters a nature zone that can truly be called Deep South. While agriculture still plays a large part in the local economy, the scenery changes. Low-lying swamps and marshes, complete with cypress trees, Spanish moss, and even an alligator or two, give a vision of subtropical splendor. In the southern part of this section, loess soil—windblown here hundreds of thousands of years ago during the Ice Age—is dominant, and its loose structure has allowed severe erosion to occur in places. Summertime heat along this section is almost unbearable, and the deep pine, live oak, and cypress forests and swamps are overrun with mosquitoes, gnats, and a thousand other varieties of insect life.

At least 100 species of trees, 215 species of birdlife, 57 species of mammals, and 89 species of reptiles and amphibians reside along today's Natchez Trace Parkway and its right-of-way. All but a handful of these are native to the region. In addition to those existing now, there once were several other magnificent species of wildlife that have been extirpated. Herds of buffalo once abounded; in fact, it is generally accepted that the origin of the Natchez Trace dates back to the time when it was a buffalo path. Elk, wolves, cougars, black bears, passenger pigeons, Carolina paraquets, and ivory-billed woodpeckers were once common all along the Trace's length.

The temperatures along the Natchez Trace, particularly in the wintertime, as well as the amount of precipitation it receives, vary almost as greatly as its plant and animal life. In modern times, average January temperatures have fluctuated by almost nine degrees between cooler Nashville and Jackson and by over eleven degrees between Nashville and Natchez. Mean July temperatures, however, among all three towns, vary by only about two degrees. The annual precipitation rate varies by almost six inches between drier Nashville and Jackson and by over ten inches between Nashville and Natchez. While temperature and precipitation patterns have almost certainly changed over the past 150 to 200 years, their degree of variation along the old Trace has, no doubt, remained essentially the same.

Today's Natchez Trace Parkway and its predecessor, the old Natchez Trace, run through some of the most picturesque countryside in the southeastern United States. The variety of plant and animal life, coupled with the differences in temperatures and rainfall along its north-south route, make the territory among the most interesting that the country has to offer.

Duck River Ridge. Pastures and farmland, mixed with deciduous woodlands, now dominate the countryside around and atop the Duck River Ridge in Middle Tennessee. As part of the Highland Rim which practically surrounds Nashville, this type of landscape is representative of the hilly topography over which the Natchez Trace runs throughout much of Tennessee. At the time the Americans discovered the convenience of the old Trace in the late 1700s, this region was largely an unbroken, primitive forest.

Photograph courtesy of the United States National Park Service

Cave Springs. The Northeast Hills of Mississippi represent the highest terrain in the state and are the westernmost extension of the southern Appalachian Mountains. The hills' limestone underpinning, like that of the Cumberland Plateau in Alabama and the Highland Rim in Tennessee, provides ideal material for the formation of caves like this one, known as Cave Springs, situated along the Natchez Trace near the Alabama–Mississippi border.

Photograph courtesy of the United States National Park Service

Forest Growth Along the Trace.
During the late 1700s, a vast
hardwood forest met the eyes
of the first American travelers
over the Natchez Trace between Nashville and the region
immediately southwest of the
Tennessee River. Although extensively logged during the last
century, much of this area today displays a second-growth
covering of many of the same
species: oak, hickory, black
walnut, tulip poplar, dogwood,
cherry, and others.

Photograph courtesy of the United States National
Park Service

Jackson Falls. The hilly topography of the Tennessee end of
the Natchez Trace created
many rapidly flowing creeks
and streams. As these watercourses tumbled over the rock
shelves of the region, water-
falls, such as this one near the
Trace's northern end, were
formed. Jackson Falls, named
in honor of General Andrew
Jackson, who passed this way
several times on journeys between his Nashville home and
the Mississippi and Louisiana
Territories, give the modern-
day traveler a glimpse of the
primeval beauty which met the
earlier wayfarer.

Photograph courtesy of the United States National
Park Service

Mid-section Forest Growth. South of the hilly, hardwood forests between Nashville and Tupelo, the Natchez Trace enters the lower-lying region representative of its middle section between Tupelo and Jackson. Here, during the days of early travel, the Trace passed through generally flat pine forests, mixed with hardwoods. This area, like the forests in Tennessee, has been extensively logged over the years, and while pine woods remain, a large portion has been devoted to agriculture.

Photograph courtesy of the United States National Park Service

Wildlife at a Salt Lick. From the names given by the early settlers to some of the rivers and streams along the Natchez Trace in Tennessee, it is evident that several species of wildlife, now extirpated, once abounded. Swan and Bear creeks and the Buffalo and Elk rivers are mute reminders of the days when their namesakes busied themselves in the forest or along waterways of the region. This old picture from a grammar school textbook depicts a buffalo and an American elk at a salt lick. These licks were common in the Middle Tennessee area and attracted wild animals, who have a natural craving for salt, from miles around.

Drawing from McGee's *History of Tennessee*

The Passenger Pigeon is the only one of a number of wildlife species now either no longer found along the Natchez Trace or extinct altogether. In 1808, Alexander Wilson, an ornithologist, spotted a single flock of pigeons in nearby Kentucky that he estimated contained more than 2 billion birds. Yet, thanks to mankind's destructiveness, this most numerous of American birds was for the most part universally exterminated by 1900. Pigeon Roost, on the Mississippi end of the Natchez Trace between Kosciusko and Tupelo, was so named because of the large number of passenger pigeons known to roost there.

Drawing by Louis Agassiz Fuertes, from a 1914 bird identification guide book

Bottomland Terrain. As the Natchez Trace pursues its southwestward course, it generally loses elevation. Mixed with the pine forests in the lower altitudes and along the stream and river bottom land are a number of marshes and swamps. Formed from backwaters on land too level to properly drain, these wet places are havens for a variety of wildlife, including muskrats, raccoons, cottontail rabbits, herons, red-winged blackbirds, and several species of snakes, turtles, and frogs.

Photograph courtesy of the United States National Park Service

Snow-covered Bridge. While the southern end of the Natchez Trace evokes visions of hot, humid conditions, this snow-covered bridge over Mississippi's Twenty-Mile Creek paints a different picture. Actually, measurable snow is almost an annual event in Mississippi and a common occurrence in Tennessee. We assume that the same general climatic conditions existed along the old Natchez Trace as do today. In the summer the heat and humidity along its southern reaches could be unbearable, while winters were usually mild.

Photograph courtesy of the United States National Park Service

Swampland Region. This swamp near Jackson is indicative of the region—typical of the Deep South—through which the Natchez Trace travels from Mississippi's capital city to Natchez. Although this particular swamp lies between Jackson and Tupelo, it really represents the more southern reaches of the Natchez Trace environment. Alligators, cottonmouth snakes, and a variety of sub-tropical wildlife inhabit this expanse, and the presence of Spanish moss hanging from the tops of the cypress trees gives an additional feeling of the warm, humid, insect-laden aspects of this southern one-third of the Trace's route.

Photograph courtesy of the United States National Park Service

The Loess Hills. As the Natchez Trace approaches the Mississippi River bluffs, it crosses the Loess Hills, a section of loose soil which runs the entire length of Mississippi from Louisiana to Tennessee. This soil was blown in by duststorms from the western plains thousands of years ago during the Ice Age, and in places it measures 90 feet thick. Loess Bluff, just outside Natchez on the Parkway, is a classic example of an exceptionally thick deposit of loess and graphically illustrates its proneness to erosion.

Photograph courtesy of the United States National Park Service

Pathway Erosion. Over the centuries, the section of the Loess Hills through which the old Natchez Trace ran could not endure the heavy traffic along the old trail. It finally gave way to the hoofprints and footprints of the countless buffalo herds and bands of humans over its loosely packed soil. Today, where the Trace crossed this unique physiographic feature, its route is marked by a deeply sunken and eroded pathway.

Photograph courtesy of the United States National Park Service

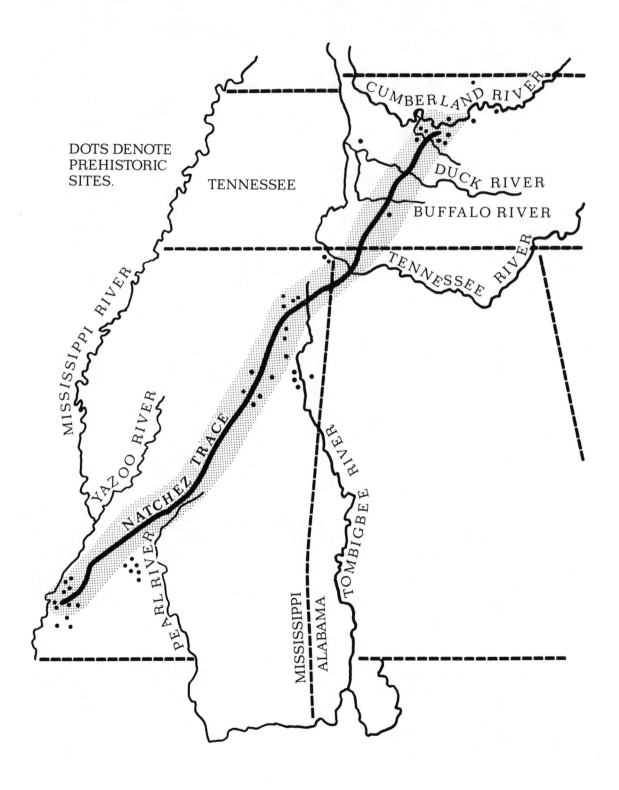

DOTS DENOTE
PREHISTORIC
SITES.

CHAPTER TWO

The Prehistoric Trace

It is now generally accepted that the first American Indians populated North America between 30 and 40 thousand years ago. While the area was dry land, these faceless wanderers crossed the Bering Strait separating Siberia from Alaska and pushed southward. Over the next several thousand years, they had settled the entire Western Hemisphere from the Arctic Circle all the way to the tip of Tierra del Fuego.

The Indians belong to the racial stock known as *Mongoloid*, and their direct ancestors lived in eastern Asia before the mass migration began across the Bering Strait. Today, while the physical features of Indians vary significantly due to thousands of years of isolation from their original homeland and from each other, they are all related to each other.

When the Indians first reached the New World, they lived very primitively. This period of prehistory, which lasted from the time of first entry from Asia until about 10,000 years ago, is called *Paleo* culture. Because of the migratory habits of these people, few cultural remains were left behind by them. Tennessee, Alabama, and Mississippi were all inhabited during this

Prehistoric Habitation Sites. There are many Prehistoric habitation sites near the Natchez Trace. The entire southeastern United States was heavily populated in aboriginal times, especially during the Mississippian period, and the region surrounding the Natchez Trace was no exception. Most of the sites portrayed on this map are Mississippian, since it was the most recent of the prehistoric periods. At the northern end of the Trace, near Nashville, according to one nineteenth century archaeologist, "the burial grounds of its aboriginal inhabitants, within a radius of thirty miles . . . contained a greater number of graves than the aggregate of the present cemeteries of the whites within the same limits." A modern counterpart has stated that more important Indian remains were found around Nashville than anywhere else in the Southeast. There can be little doubt that as communications and travel were established among the various Indian groups in the region, a sophisticated trail system evolved. The forerunner of the Natchez Trace was not only the link between the villages around Nashville and those in the south near Natchez, but was also part of a larger highway network connecting villages throughout the eastern United States.

Drawing by James A. Crutchfield and Edison Travelstead

time, however, and evidence of Paleo culture, primarily in the form of fluted spear points, has been found in a number of locations in all three states.

Paleo times were dominated by bands of hunters, who wandered from place to place in search of the wild animal herds upon which they depended for subsistence. The diet consisted overwhelmingly of meat, as in all hunting cultures. Perhaps wild berries were eaten now and then, but it was not until many years later that fruit and vegetable gathering supplemented the largely protein diet. No village life existed, and no permanent forms of housing were used. Improvisation was the watchword, and any convenient rock overhang or cave sufficed for shelter. This wandering spirit precluded any stabilization of domestic life, and consequently Paleo hunters and their families reached no great degree of advancement over that of a purely hunting society.

New influences from Asia around 10,000 years ago introduced ideas that somewhat modified the nomadic hunting traits of the Paleo people. The period called *Archaic* brought with it the beginnings of settled life. Primitive forms of agriculture, although practiced on a small scale, became apparent, and fish supplemented the still largely meat diet of these technologically advanced newcomers. Hunting continued to maintain its position as the primary occupation for Archaic men, but the introduction of the *atlatl,* or spear-thrower, greatly facilitated this laborious and dangerous pursuit.

The atlatl was a small piece of curved wood that, when attached to the hand-held end of the spear shaft, allowed a much more powerful thrust to be generated by the human thrower. Although this was a modest improvement when judged by today's standards, this progress in weapon technology gave the Archaic hunter and warrior a decided advantage over his Paleo ancestor. The increased use of the atlatl, along with the advent of the rudiments of agriculture, the use of fish as a variation in the diet, and the beginnings of a primitive trade network all contributed to making life a little easier for Archaic people when compared to their Paleo predecessors.

Archaic times were followed around 3000 years ago by the *Woodland* period. The village life begun earlier was maintained and expanded, and agriculture became more important in the daily lives of the Woodland people. Hunting was still pursued, but by this time a modest spectrum of farm produce was available. No evidence of Woodland architecture has survived, but from post-mold arrangements in known village sites, archaeologists have deduced that the houses of the times were probably built of bark and tree limbs spread over an arrangement of upright poles, set in the ground in a circular or elliptical pattern.

Pottery was introduced during Woodland times, and while not the beautifully designed and executed handicrafts of a later age, it sufficed for its intended uses—cooking and storage. The bow-and-arrow gradually replaced the spear and atlatl as the primary hunting and defense weapon. A growing cult centered around burial practices was another new feature of the Woodland culture. Sometimes called mound builders, the people of this period developed the custom of burying the dead under mounds of earth, the soil being laboriously carried by the village inhabitants and heaped, one load upon another, until the desired height was obtained.

Sometime around 700 A.D., the *Mississippian* culture became prominent across the entire southeastern United States. Massive earthen temple mounds were built, each requiring thousands of hours of back-breaking labor. Defensive works, consisting of stockades and watchtowers, surrounded towns and villages many acres in size. Beautiful pottery, statues, and ceremonial objects were created. Agriculture was practiced on a large-scale basis, and a sophisticated network of trade, linking villages separated by hundreds of miles of wilderness, was established.

Because of the durability of many of the temple mounds and other material artifacts—and also because it is becoming increasingly evident that Mississippian culture was still active, though waning, at the time of the first European contact in the region—the life and times of the Mississippian people are better understood than any other southeastern prehistoric culture. The area along the Natchez Trace contains many examples of Mississippian villages and mounds, and, in fact, the old Trace itself was no doubt used as a trade highway connecting villages on the Cumberland River in Tennessee with those in central and southwestern Mississippi.

By the seventeenth century, the fires of Mississippian brilliance were rapidly becoming extinguished. The towns lay deserted, the mounds fell into disrepair, and the artifacts became lost in the soil for future archaeologists to find. It now appears entirely possible that when De Soto explored the southeastern United States in the 1540s—including a direct crossing of the Natchez Trace in present-day Mississippi—he and his party witnessed the last days of Mississippian culture. It was not much later, however, that the Historic tribes—the Cherokees, Chickasaws, Choctaws, Shawnees, and Natchez—gained ascendancy over the entire region. With their appearance, the Prehistoric era was over, and the Historic period began.

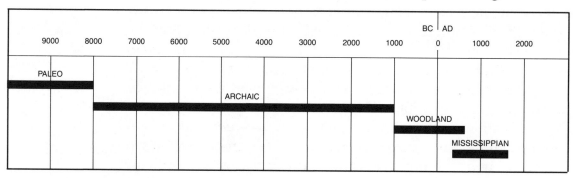

Ancient Indian Cultures. The Prehistoric population of the southeastern United States fell into four major groups: Paleo, Archaic, Woodland, and Mississippian. The oldest culture, Paleo, was purely hunting in nature and persisted for several thousand years. We know that Paleo hunters were present in the region from the many fluted spear points, the predominant handiwork of the period, which have been found in Tennessee, Alabama, and Mississippi. The transition from Paleo to Archaic occurred about 10,000 years ago. The new people practiced a crude form of agriculture and they lived in villages instead of constantly wandering about like their predecessors. The village life which began in Archaic times became more common during the Woodland Period, which had its beginnings about 3000 years ago. Because of their custom of burying the dead in mounds, the Woodland people are sometimes called Mound Builders. Pottery was introduced in this period and the bow and arrow became the primary weapon. Around 700 A.D., Mississippian culture became dominant. Large temple mounds, stockades, and watchtowers became popular, and the once-small villages of past years grew into large towns many acres in size. Handicrafts reached a new level of beauty. The Mississippian and Historic periods merged around 1600 A.D., and by the time post-De Soto contact was made, the area was in the process of being taken over by several Historic Indian tribes, among them the Natchez, Choctaw, Chickasaw, Cherokee, and Shawnee.

Pharr Mound Stockade. These post holes at the Pharr Mound site outline the stockade which once protected the village here. While Woodland burials at the location have been dated as early as 200 A.D., it is estimated that the village and stockade ruins existed later, around 1000 A.D. If the latter date is correct, it appears that this site was continuously occupied from at least Woodland times on into the Mississippian era. Settlement at one location by people of several culture groups is not an uncommon feature of many archaeological sites, since the earlier people are seldom completely wiped out by their cultural conquerors. On the contrary, fresh ideas and ideals—in other words, new culture—are gradually disseminated to the established people of an area by the newcomers, so that over a period of many years these ideas are really no longer foreign. To succeeding generations, it is just as if these customs had been present all along. Thus, by *acculturation* and *assimilation*, the new ideas are no longer considered new and find niches in the culture of the old, established lifestyle.

Photograph courtesy of the United States National Park Service

The Bear Creek Mound is not only the oldest major Prehistoric site along the Natchez Trace, but is probably one of the few that was occupied over several thousand years—from Paleo times all the way through the Mississippian period. Located near the Mississippi–Alabama border, the existing mound measures about ten feet high and displays the typical flat top of a temple mound.

Photograph courtesy of the United States National Park Service

Pharr Mound Site. One of the eight mounds which have been excavated at the Pharr Mound site looms above a recently cultivated field. Dating from Woodland times, the Pharr Mounds and their dependent territory cover more than ninety acres near the Natchez Trace in northern Mississippi.

Photograph courtesy of the United States National Park Service

Village Life at Bynum. The Bynum Mounds, located on the Natchez Trace about thirty-four miles southwest of Tupelo, are part of a Woodland site which originally included a village, six burial mounds, and dependent fields and gardens. Today only two mounds, each about 10 feet high, are readily visible. The painting shows what village life was like at Bynum during its heyday. In later years the site was settled by Historic Chickasaw Indians.

Photograph courtesy of the United States National Park Service

Bynum Artifacts. Artifacts found in the mounds unearthed by National Park archaeologists in 1948 provide evidence that the Bynum people had developed a vast trade network, no doubt using the Natchez Trace as their main north–south artery. Flint from Ohio, green stone from Tennessee, shells from the Gulf Coast, and copper from the Lake Superior region were a few of the imported items that gave these Woodland folks the raw materials which they needed in everyday life.

Photograph courtesy of the United States National Park Service

A Bynum Mound Today.

Photograph by Regena H. Crutchfield

Boyd Mounds. Also settled by Woodland people was the village located near the Boyd Mounds, just north of Jackson. The one mound that is visible today is only five feet high, but stretches more than one hundred feet in length.

Photograph courtesy of the United States National Park Service

Boyd Village Life. An artist's drawing of Boyd village life shows a modest townsite, partially surrounded by a stockade. The young boy on the left holds a bow, the most popular weapon of the times, while an older woman, in the middle background, scrapes corn, a product already heavily relied upon by Woodland people everywhere.

Photograph courtesy of the United States National Park Service

Emerald Mound. As the Woodland period slipped into the Mississippian era, the concept of the once small burial mound suddenly underwent a dramatic change. Large, flat-topped temple mounds became popular, and while the smaller burial mounds were still used for their original purposes, these more massive, ceremonial platforms became the center of Mississippian village life. Emerald Mound, just north of Natchez, covers almost eight acres, is the third largest mound in the United States, and was the religious center for outlying villages and towns.

Photograph courtesy of the United States National Park Service

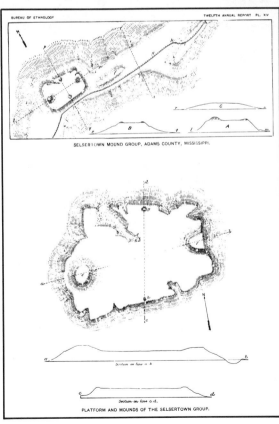

BUREAU OF ETHNOLOGY   TWELFTH ANNUAL REPORT PL. XIV

SELSERTOWN MOUND GROUP, ADAMS COUNTY, MISSISSIPPI.

PLATFORM AND MOUNDS OF THE SELSERTOWN GROUP.

Selsertown Mounds. Until the 1930s and 1940s, the Emerald Mound complex was known as the Selsertown Mounds. Named after the nearby, now extinct, village of Selsertown—a site which itself had a role in Natchez Trace history as an early way station and post office—the mounds were explored by the Cyrus Thomas Party for the Bureau of American Ethnology in 1884 and again in 1887. The party's findings, along with this plate, were published in 1894 as part of the Twelfth Annual Report of the Bureau.

Drawing from the Twelfth Annual Report of The Bureau of American Ethnology

The Mound Bottom site along the Harpeth River west of Nashville was one of the largest Prehistoric complexes in the entire Southeast. The two separate areas of this site—one known as Mound Bottom and the other called Mound City—are separated from each other by about one mile, and when taken together, cover over 500 acres. It was once assumed that the entire complex was inhabited at the same time, but it is currently believed that, while both divisions date from Missis-sippian times, they may not have been occupied simultaneously. The Mound Bottom division, shown at right, is owned by the Tennessee Department of Conservation and is in the process of being restored to its original appearance as an archaeological park. Photo at left shows the outline of a Mound Bottom Mississippian period house during excavation in 1974 by Tennessee Archaeology Division scientists.

Photographs courtesy of the Tennessee Department of Conservation Division of Archaeology

Emerald Mound. Atop the flat-surfaced platform at Emerald Mound, there were originally eleven smaller mounds. When the Thomas party explored the area, its archaeologists could find only four, and today only two—one on either end of the east–west axis—are readily visible. The largest mound, shown here, probably served as the base for a temple or for a chief's residence, while other ceremonial buildings were placed in the plaza in the foreground. It is estimated that Emerald Mound was built between 1300 and 1600 A.D., and some authorities believe it was still occupied by Mississippian people when the first white contact was made in these parts.

Photograph courtesy of the United States National Park Service

Temple Mound. The Mound City division of Mound Bottom contained this temple mound which dominated one corner of a large plaza measuring about 500 by 1000 feet. The Harpeth River and its steep bluffs protected two sides of the site, while an earthen embankment, topped by a wooden stockade, ran along the other two sides. Watch towers were placed every few yards along the stockade. Several other plazas and mounds were also included in this division. The photo, taken in 1936, clearly shows the ancient mound silhouetted against the horizon.

Photograph courtesy of the University of Tennessee Frank H. McClung Museum

A Mississippian town during its height of occupation probably looked much like this diorama at the Mound State Monument in Alabama. The largest of the flat-topped mounds held the temple, or maybe the house of the chief, while the smaller ones served as platforms for less important buildings. The villagers' houses were scattered across the rest of the complex, and the fields of corn and beans lay beyond the town.

West Harpeth Site. Visible today on State Highway 96, between Franklin, Tennessee, and the route of the soon-to-be completed Natchez Trace Parkway, is the West Harpeth site. Privately owned and currently under cultivation, the two mounds can still be clearly seen just off the road. This village site, on the banks of the West Harpeth River, originally contained about seven acres, and was surrounded by earthworks some 1,970 feet long.

Photograph by Regena H. Crutchfield

Old Town. Another Mississippian site located near the Natchez Trace in Middle Tennessee is Old Town. The village located here covered twelve acres and was protected by earthworks and palisades stretching for 2,500 feet. The two temple mounds, while once much higher, can barely be seen rising above the pasture in the foreground. The burial mound, also much smaller than originally, is only slightly visible today.

Photograph by Regena H. Crutchfield

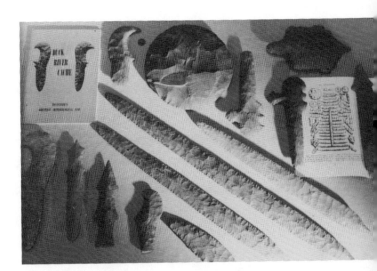

Mississippian Ceremonial Pottery. Flint work was not the only area of handicrafts in which the Mississippian people excelled. These examples of ceremonial pottery unearthed in the Nashville area during the last century show a high degree of skill. They also reveal an advanced civilization—one that allowed a class of artisans to pursue its interests, while other classes of farmers and workmen provided food for the entire community, including those members engaged in non-essential occupations. The Mississippians' handicrafts, their mound building abilities, and their high degree of ceremonial participation all contributed to the evolution of a culture which was as advanced for this part of North America as the Aztec and Maya cultures were for Central America. In fact, some authorities maintain that influences from the Valley of Mexico were largely responsible for the high degree of civilization among the Mississippian peoples, as well as for some of their similarities with the Central American empires.

Photograph from the Twentieth Annual Report of the Bureau of American Ethnology

Duck River Artifacts. The fine craftsmanship of the Mississippian people is evident in these artifacts discovered years ago along the Duck River in Tennessee. This exquisite find of symbolic flint objects included a finely chipped "sword" which measured almost twenty-eight inches long. One contemporary archaeologist has described the objects as "some of the most extraordinary flint work ever made by man. . . ." The Duck River collection provides additional insight into the vast trade network maintained by the Mississippian people, including the use of the Natchez Trace, since objects produced by Duck River artisans have been found in sites all over the South.

Photograph courtesy of the Tennessee Department of Conservation

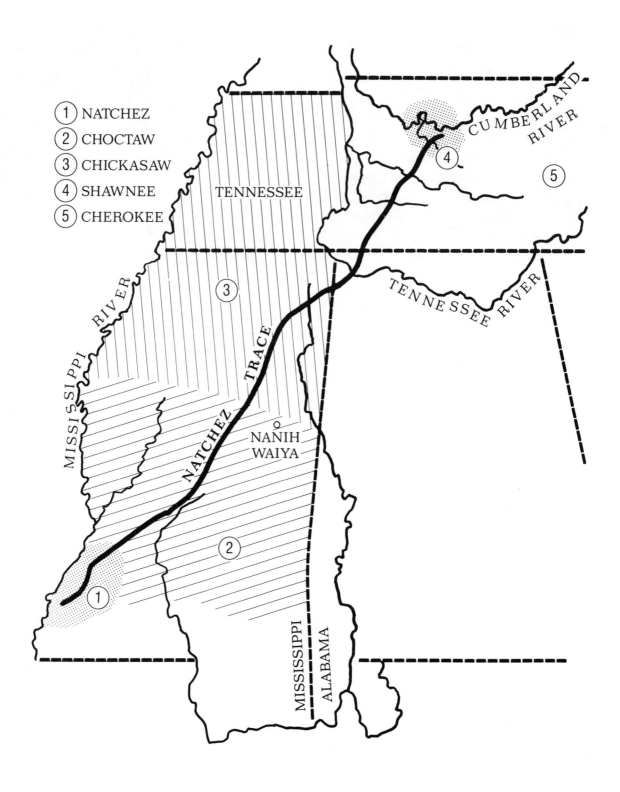

1 NATCHEZ
2 CHOCTAW
3 CHICKASAW
4 SHAWNEE
5 CHEROKEE

TENNESSEE

CUMBERLAND RIVER

MISSISSIPPI RIVER

NATCHEZ TRACE

TENNESSEE RIVER

NANIH WAIYA

MISSISSIPPI

ALABAMA

CHAPTER THREE

Indian Trails

There is not a precise time to which historians can point as being the end of the Mississippian period and the beginning of the Historic period. Normally, that transition is thought to have occurred at about the time that first European contact was made with the native population of the Southeast; i.e., in the middle of the sixteenth century. Indeed, as mentioned in the last chapter, Mississippian culture was very likely in its final days of decline when De Soto explored parts of Tennessee, Alabama, and Mississippi in the 1540s.

As mysterious as the timing of the two periods' transmutation is the cause of the change. Why did a society so far advanced in agriculture, ceremonial ritual, and handicrafts suddenly disappear to be replaced by a less sophisticated population? What happened to the driving force of the Mississippian people—the force responsible for the construction of towns scores of acres in size, the creation of flint and pottery objects as artistically perfect as any ever created by man, and the establishment of a trade network that linked villages all over the eastern United States?

While the *exact* cause of the replacement of Mississippian

Indian Tribes along the Trace. The region lying along the Natchez Trace was inhabited in historic times by three major tribes of American Indian. The Natchez tribe lived in the southwestern extremity of the area near the present-day city of Natchez, Mississippi. The Choctaw and Chickasaw peoples claimed the rest of the state, the Choctaws the southern part and the Chickasaws the northern end. The Chickasaws also claimed, but did not occupy, western Tennessee and western Kentucky. Chickasaw Bluffs, on the site of today's Memphis, was used as a place of embarkation and debarkation for the Chickasaws in their journeys up and down the Mississippi River, and a trail connected that point and their villages around present-day Tupelo. The Cherokees claimed—but maintained no villages in—Middle Tennessee around the Nashville area. The Shawnee tribe established a town along the Cumberland River on the site of Nashville, but was driven out in the early 1700s by a joint Chickasaw–Cherokee war party.

Drawing by James A. Crutchfield and Edison Travelstead

traditions with those of the Historic Indian tribes eludes us, it is known that the mechanism of the change was *assimilation* and not conquest by a different group. Unlike the Aztecs of Mexico, or the Incas of Peru, who both were subdued by the Spanish, there is no indication of direct confrontation between the Mississippians and more recently immigrated peoples. On the contrary, the inhabitants of the Southeast simply ceased their grandiose building and the pursuit of their other sophisticated life styles and, over a period of years, gradually modified their older attitudes and folkways into the newer style of living that we associate today with the Historic tribes of Indians.

Most of the Historic Indian population inhabiting the region through which the Natchez Trace passed belonged to one or the other of three tribes, all native to present-day Mississippi. The Natchez tribe lived in the southwestern portion of the state, around the city which today bears its name. The Choctaw people had settled in the southern and middle parts of Mississippi, while the Chickasaws, although their villages were centered in the Tupelo area, claimed the northern section, as well as most of western Tennessee and Kentucky. The Tennessee end of the Natchez Trace went through territory which was claimed by the Cherokees, although in Historic times the region was largely uninhabited, except for a small colony of Shawnees who lived around the future site of Nashville in the early 1700s.

Linguistically, all three of the tribes were related. They were members of the great Muskhogean language group, which was the predominant tongue among the Indians of the southeastern United States. The most aberrant of the three, the Natchez was for years mistakenly thought to have spoken a dialect totally distinct from all other American Indians, but later research has proven that it, too, fell within the Muskhogean fold. Other well known tribes belonging to this group are the Creek, Alabama, and Seminole.

The southernmost of the three, the Natchez, is today an extinct tribe. Never extremely large, it probably numbered around 4000 to 4,500 in 1650. The tribe maintained the most advanced culture of any of the southeastern Indians—a culture which no doubt was a direct descendant of the Mississippian

tradition of prehistoric times. Indeed, theirs was the most sophisticated civilization north of the Aztecs and Mayas of Mexico and Central America. The Natchez were accomplished
farmers and skilled artisans. Much like the proud Mississippians, they were oriented toward great ceremonialism and maintained the temple mound concept right down to the coming of
the white man.

A class conscious people, the Natchez tribe was divided
into four classes: suns, nobles, honored people, and stinkards,
or commoners. Strict rules were followed as to which class
could marry into which. The chief, or Great Sun, held absolute
power over his subjects, and when he died, his wives were
strangled and laid to rest with him for his afterlife pleasure.
When the Natchez were finally crushed by the Europeans, the
last vestiges of the once-brilliant Mississippian culture disap-
peared forever.

The Choctaws and Chickasaws were very closely related,
although throughout their existence, they maintained an enmity
toward one another unparalleled in Indian history. Both tribes'
traditions relate that when their people were one, they migrated
to the Mississippi region from somewhere to the west. Once in
the "promised land" they separated—at a spot called "Nanih
Waiya," the hill of origins—and the two tribes claimed their respective territories and hated each other from then on.

The more southern Choctaw numbered around 15,000 people in 1650 and was the second most populous tribe in the
Southeast, being surpassed only by the Cherokees. They were a
predominantly peaceful, agricultural tribe. Through influences from their older neighbors, they took up the tradition of
flattening their infants' heads, and consequently were known
to the early French as "Flatheads." Choctaw men also wore
their hair long, a habit not shared by most of the surrounding
tribes. Another custom was the employment by the bereaved of
professional "bone-pickers." Bone-pickers' with long finger-
nails to facilitate their work, would be summoned to climb a
burial platform and to pick the flesh from decayed corpses.
The flesh would be burned, while the bones were placed in a
coffin. This grisly tradition appears to have been unique to the
Choctaws—at least among the other southeastern tribes.

The Chickasaws, about half as numerous in 1650 as their Choctaw brethren, were exact opposites. Restless hunters who frowned on farming and the settled village life of their neighbors, they were among the fiercest fighters in North America. "The most intrepid warriors of the South" is how one historian has described the Chickasaws, while another points out that they were "noted from remote times for their bravery, independence, and warlike disposition."

When the Spanish explorer Hernando De Soto traveled through the southeastern United States in the early 1540s, he was the first documented white man to ever come into contact with several Indian tribes, including the Choctaw and the Chickasaw. It is likely that De Soto's followers, after his death, were the first to see the Natchez as well. From the time these initial contacts were made, Indian culture in the Southeast was changed forever. Regardless of how modest this first meeting of the two diverse cultures was, the continued influence of the white man upon the Indian was the single most important element in the long decline of the red man in America.

Grand Natchez Mounds. By modern times, the Grand Village of the Natchez had become overgrown with forest. Located just outside the city of Natchez on the banks of St. Catherine Creek, this site was once known as the Fatherland Plantation Mounds. In 1703, a French visitor recorded: "This nation is composed of thirty villages, but the one we visited was the largest, because it contained the dwelling of the Great Chief, whom they called the Sun, which means noble." This photograph shows a Grand Natchez mound in 1940.

Photograph courtesy of the United States National Park Service

The Grand Village of the Natchez is restored and maintained by the Mississippi Department of Archives and History. Archaeological investigations were conducted at the site in 1930, 1962, 1972, and 1973, and most of the present knowledge about the capital of the Natchez tribe has been derived from these scientific explorations and the journals of early visitors to the town. One of the village's mounds is shown here as it appears today.
Photograph by Regena H. Crutchfield

A typical Natchez house at the Grand Village appeared much the same as this modern-day reconstruction. The walls were of wattle-and-daub construction, and the roof was made of straw thatch. The normally warm winters made elaborate housing unnecessary, and the hot summers demanded insulation from the intense heat.
Photograph by Regena H. Crutchfield

Funeral at Grand Natchez. The main mound at the Grand Village of the Natchez during a funeral ceremony probably looked much like this artist's reconstruction. The occasion is the funeral of White Woman, the mother of the Great Sun. The Great Sun himself stands atop the main mound, while White Woman's house burns, according to tradition, on a distant mound. The husband of White Woman, lying beside her on the bier, has already been strangled to death and will join his wife in the glorious afterlife which awaits them.
Picture reproduced from *America's Fascinating Indian Heritage*, © 1978, The Reader's Digest Association, Inc. Used by permission.

a Summer clothing of a Natchez man   b Winter clothing of a Natchez man   c Clothing of a Natchez woman and girl

Clothing of the Natchez Indians. Most of the remaining information in this chapter regarding the Historic tribes' customs and traditions is derived from the reports of white observers, and these journals are all that history has with which to reconstruct the tribes' lifestyles as they were in the years immediately preceding white contact. We can only assume that enough of the traditions were still present when the whites arrived to have allowed them to document the Indians' ancient ways accurately. Much of what we know today about the Natchez tribe is derived from the writings of Antoine Le Page du Pratz. This Frenchman lived among the Natchez in the 1720s, and in 1758 he published a book entitled *Histoirie de La Louisiana* which gave many valuable descriptions and pictures of the Natchez people and their way of life. Regarding Natchez clothing, du Pratz said, "During the hot season the men wear only a breechcloth. This is the skin of a deer dressed white or dyed black, but few except chiefs wear breechcloths of black skin. . . . When it is cold the men cover themselves with a shirt made of two dressed deerskins, which resembles rather a nightgown than a shirt, the sleeves having only such length as the breadth of the skin permits. . . . The women in the warm season wear only half an ell of *Limbourg* (cloth), with which they cover themselves. They wind this cloth about their bodies, and are well covered from the belt to the knees. . . . With women as with men, the remainder of the body is uncovered."

Pictures from Bulletin 43 of the Bureau of American Ethnology

The Great Sun of the Natchez was the supreme chief of all the people and held absolute control over the affairs of the tribe. This drawing from du Pratz shows the Great Sun being carried to a feast in a litter "composed of four red bars which cross each other at the far corners of the seat, which has a depth of about 1½ feet. . . . Those who prepare this conveyance are the first and the oldest warriors of the nation."

Picture from Bulletin 43 of the Bureau of American Ethnology

Tattooed Serpent's Funeral. The Tattooed Serpent was the war chief of the Natchez Indians, and, when du Pratz was living among the tribe in 1725, was also the brother of the Great Sun. Du Pratz witnessed the Tattooed Serpent's death and the ensuing funeral ceremonies, which, to say the least, were elaborate. In this picture the Tattooed Serpent is being carried to the temple by the shrine's guardians. In a few moments, his wives and other household members will be strangled to death.

Picture from Bulletin 43 of the Bureau of American Ethnology

Natchez Prisoner Executions. The Natchez were ruthless adversaries in war. Du Pratz indicated that if male prisoners are taken, the Natchez warriors "go at once to hunt for the three poles which are necessary for the construction of the fatal instrument on which they are going to make the enemy they have taken die. I mean the frame on which they cruelly immolate the unfortunate victim of their vengeance." After the prisoner's final meal, the warrior who actually captured him "gives a blow of his wooden war club below the back part of his head, making the death cry. Having thus stunned him he cuts the skin around his hair, puts his knees on his forehead, takes his hair in both hands, pulls it from the skull, and makes the death cry while removing the scalp in the best manner he is able without tearing it." A long, agonizing death usually followed, sometimes taking up to three days and three nights, with the victim being burned slowly about his body until life finally escaped him.

Picture from Bulletin 43 of the Bureau of American Ethnology

Natchez Harvest Dance. During the harvest feast of the Natchez, dancing was a common pastime. In describing this activity, du Pratz reported that an open space "is surrounded with more than two hundred torches made of dried canes, which they take care to renew. . . . In the great light which they shed, they dance ordinarily until day. The dances are always the same, and he who has seen one has seen all."

Picture from Bulletin 43 of the Bureau of American Ethnology

Choctaw Funeral Place. In his 1775 study entitled *A Concise Natural History of East and West Florida,* Bernard Romans left a picture and description of a Choctaw funeral place. "As soon as the deceased is departed," he wrote, "a stage is erected, and the corpse is laid on it and covered with a bear skin; if he be a man of note, it is decorated, and the poles painted red with vermillion and bear's oil; if a child, it is put upon stakes set across; at this stage the relations come and weep, asking many questions of the corpse, such as, why he left them?" Months after the ceremony, the "bone-pickers," described earlier, completed their gruesome work before depositing the victim "to lasting oblivion."

Picture from Bulletin 137 of the Bureau of American Ethnology

Choctaw Warriors. Another Frenchman who helped preserve southeastern Indian history and customs is A. De Batz. A draftsman by profession, De Batz was responsible for many drawings which vividly portray everyday life among several tribes during the eighteenth century. This one shows two Choctaw warriors carrying scalps, while children play at their feet, apparently untouched by the grisly scene before them. Note that the one brave already boasts a European introduction, the powder horn.

Picture from Bulletin 137 of the Bureau of American Ethnology

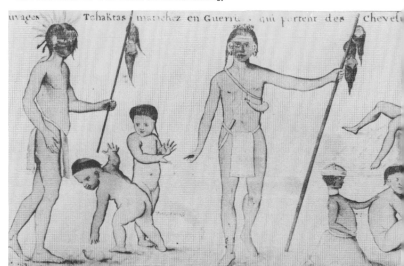

Choctaw Stickball Game. The Choctaws were great ball players. The game which they played is today commonly called lacross, and it was a favorite among most of the tribes of the southeastern United States. Among the Choctaws, however, there was one peculiarity. After the men had played the game to their satisfaction, the women were allowed to play. Women players were apparently not permitted in other tribes. Reports throughout the years indicate that each ball team employed anywhere from twenty to over one hundred players. In any event, "stickball," as it was called among the Choctaw tribe, was an extremely rough sport with broken arms and legs common occurrences, and once in a while a life was lost. This picture by George Catlin shows a Choctaw stickball game in full progress. Although the drawing dates from the time that the Choctaws had already moved west of the Mississippi River, it no doubt represents the game as it was played in their ancient homeland along the Natchez Trace as well.

Photograph of the George Catlin lithograph courtesy of Les Leverett

Choctaw Ball Player. George Catlin's illustration of a Choctaw ball player vividly portrays the social significance given to the sport, as represented by the man's fine attire. It also shows the two sticks used by the southeastern tribes as opposed to the single stick of the Great Lakes people. During his single-handed mission of documenting the American Indian, Catlin wrote that he "made it a uniform rule whilst in the Indian country, to attend every ball-play I could hear of, if I could do it by riding a distance of twenty or thirty miles . . . and look on . . . with irresistable laughter at the succession of tricks, and kicks and scuffles which ensue, in the almost super-human struggle for the ball."

Photograph of the George Catlin lithograph courtesy of Les Leverett

Modern Choctaw Ball Players. Stickballing is still a favorite sport among the Choctaws living on the reservation near Philadelphia, Mississippi.

Photograph courtesy of the United States National Park Service

THE

HISTORY

OF THE

AMERICAN INDIANS,

PARTICULARLY

THOSE NATIONS ADJOINING TO THE MISSISSIPPI, EAST AND WEST FLOR
IDA, GEORGIA, SOUTH AND NORTH CAROLINA, AND VIRGINIA

CONTAINING

AN ACCOUNT OF THEIR ORIGIN, LANGUAGE, MANNERS, RELIGIOUS AND
CIVIL CUSTOMS, LAWS, FORM OF GOVERNMENT, PUNISHMENTS,
CONDUCT IN WAR AND DOMESTIC LIFE, THEIR HABITS,
DIET, AGRICULTURE, MANUFACTURES, DIS
EASES AND METHOD OF CURE, AND
OTHER PARTICULARS, SUFFI
CIENT TO RENDER IT

A COMPLETE INDIAN SYSTEM,

WITH

OBSERVATIONS ON FORMER HISTORIANS, THE CONDUCT OF OUR COLONY
GOVERNORS, SUPERINTENDENTS, MISSIONARIES, &C

ALSO

AN APPENDIX

CONTAINING

A DESCRIPTION OF THE FLORIDAS AND THE MISSISSIPPI LANDS, WITH
THEIR PRODUCTIONS, THE BENEFITS OF COLONIZING GEORGIANA
AND CIVILIZING THE INDIANS, AND THE WAY TO MAKE
ALL THE COLONIES MORE VALUABLE TO THE
MOTHER COUNTRY.

WITH A NEW MAP OF THE COUNTRY REFERRED TO IN THE HISTORY.

BY JAMES ADAIR, ESQUIRE.

A TRADER WITH THE INDIANS, AND RESIDENT IN THEIR COUNTRY FOR FORTY YEARS.

LONDON:

PRINTED FOR EDWARD AND CHARLES DILLY, IN THE POULTRY.

MDCCLXXV.

The History of the American Indians. James Adair, a trader among the southern Indians, was born about 1709 in County Antrim, Ireland. Later migrating to America, Adair traded extensively with the Cherokees during the late 1730s and early 1740s. In 1744, he moved to the Chickasaw nation and set up a trade relationship with members of that tribe, and, a little later, with the Choctaws. Adair was a firm advocate of the theory that all American Indians were descended from the Lost Tribes of Israel, a common belief in his time. The arguments for his convictions were recorded in his book, *The History of the American Indians,* published in London in 1775. Although he was wrong about the Indians' descent, his descriptions of the Chickasaws, Choctaws, and other southern tribes are a valuable source of information. Pictured is the title page from Adair's book, an item that today is treasured by collectors.
From the Author's collection

Nanih Waiya. At a place called "Nanih Waiya," the hill of origins, the Choctaws and the Chickasaws parted company and became separate tribal entities. Nanih Waiya is located in Winston County, Mississippi, not far from the Natchez Trace.
Picture from Bulletin 137 of the Bureau of American Ethnology

A Chickasaw Town. While the Chickasaws settled into a relatively small area and clustered their villages, old writings would lead us to believe that there was at least some autonomy among the individual parts of the settlements making up a town. One early writer, after referring to "what might be called one town, or rather an assemblage of huts, of the length of about one mile and a half," reports that this conglomeration was divided into seven entities. This structure is consistent with the Chickasaws preference for the wide open spaces.

Photograph of U.S. Park Service Panorama by Regena H. Crutchfield

Winter House

Chickasaw Winter House. James Adair lived among the Chickasaws for several years, and his account of their housing has allowed a National Park artist to reconstruct this aspect of everyday life. "The clothing of the Indians being very light," reported Adair, "they provide themselves for the winter with hot-houses, whose properties are to retain and reflect the heat, after the manner of the Dutch stoves. . . . The door of this winter palace, is commonly about four feet high, and so narrow as not to admit two to enter it abreast, with a winding passage for the space of six or seven feet to secure themselves both from the power of bleak winds, and of an invading enemy." These circular houses measured about 24 feet in diameter.

Photograph courtesy of the United States National Park Service

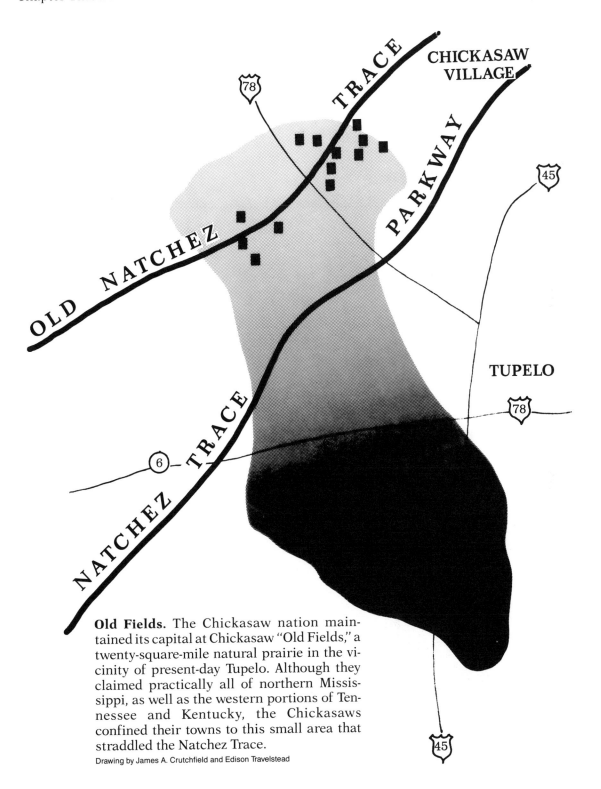

Old Fields. The Chickasaw nation maintained its capital at Chickasaw "Old Fields," a twenty-square-mile natural prairie in the vicinity of present-day Tupelo. Although they claimed practically all of northern Mississippi, as well as the western portions of Tennessee and Kentucky, the Chickasaws confined their towns to this small area that straddled the Natchez Trace.

Drawing by James A. Crutchfield and Edison Travelstead

Chickasaw Summer House.
"For their summer house, they generally fix strong posts of pitch-pine deep in the ground, which will last for several ages. The trees of dried locust and sassafras, are likewise very durable," Adair reported in his book. Rectangular in design and measuring about thirteen by thirty-five feet, the pine or cypress walls were so durable that they were bullet-proof. "They finish this summer house of pleasure, without any kind of iron, or working tools whatsoever, except a small hatchet of iron (that formerly was a long sharpened stone) and a knife. . . ," related Adair.

Photograph courtesy of the United States National Park Service

A Characteristic Chickasaw Indian Head.
Only one artistic representation of a Chickasaw Indian has passed down to us from the early days of this tribe's settlement in northern Mississippi. This drawing, which appeared in Bernard Romans' *A Concise Natural History of East and West Florida*, is entitled "A Characteristic Chickasaw Head," and is probably a fairly accurate portrayal of Chickasaw features. According to one modern-day historian, the Chickasaws lost their tribal purity at an early date, and by colonial times very few pure-blooded Indians of this tribe could be located.

Picture from Bulletin 137 of the Bureau of American Ethnology

Chickasaw Fort. Forts were common among many southeastern Indian tribes, and evidence of their existence has been verified in the remains of many prehistoric cultures as well as in the chronicles of De Soto, which frequently mentions them at a time before white contact could have introduced the idea. Most of the Chickasaw towns in Historic times were probably protected by some kind of rough stockade to which the people could flee in the event of an attack. Built of high logs set at close intervals in the ground, the typical Chickasaw fort measured about eighty-five by sixty-eight feet and had overlapping entrances on both short sides. Along the inside perimeter of the wall was a ditch in which the men could stand and fire through ground level openings in the palisades. Before the introduction of firearms by Europeans, it would seem more likely that a more upright firing position—from which to shoot a bow and arrow—would have been used.

Fort

Photograph courtesy of the United States National Park Service

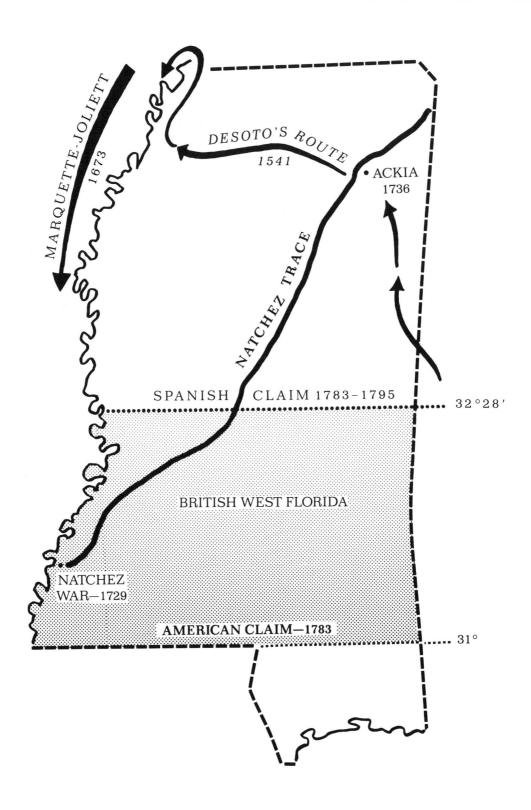

MARQUETTE-JOLIETT
1673

DESOTO'S ROUTE
1541

• ACKIA
1736

NATCHEZ TRACE

SPANISH   CLAIM 1783-1795   ····· 32°28′

BRITISH WEST FLORIDA

NATCHEZ
WAR—1729

AMERICAN CLAIM—1783   ····· 31°

CHAPTER FOUR

European Contact in the South

Hernando De Soto's abrupt appearance in Florida in 1539 and his army's explorations over the next three years of much of the southeastern section of the United States signaled the beginning of the end for the native Indian population throughout the region. Although it would be many more years before several of the tribes encountered by De Soto would ever see another white man, the effects of the initial clash with the Spaniards were both profound and permanent. As technologically advanced as some of the southeastern Indians were, the arrival in their midst of bearded white men with shining armor, horses, cattle, and firearms was a spectacle they would not soon forget.

After De Soto, the Frenchmen Marquette and Joliett were the next whites to visit the Indians in the Mississippi Valley. Descending the Mississippi River in 1673 as far south as the mouth of the Arkansas River north of present-day Greenville, Mississippi, they were followed in 1682 by their countryman,

---

European Possession of Natchez Trace. Before the United States finally took physical possession of the area in 1798, the flags of France, Great Britain, and Spain had all flown over Natchez and the surrounding countryside. By right of La Salle's French claim over the Mississippi Valley in 1682, the entire area from Natchez to Nashville was unofficially French. Losing the territory to Great Britain at the close of the French and Indian War, France was never again a meaningful power in America. At the same time that England acquired France's possessions, it obtained one of Spain's colonies, Spanish Florida, covering roughly today's state of the same name. Consolidating the two pieces of real estate, the British Crown created its own West Florida, which took up the southern one-third of present-day Mississippi, Alabama, and part of the panhandle of Florida. When Spain re-occupied Natchez during the American Revolution, it took over West Florida. At the close of the War, the region eventually went to the United States, but not until after several years of debate with the Spanish about the location of the southern boundary line.

Drawing by James A. Crutchfield and Edison Travelstead

Robert Cavelier, sieur de la Salle. La Salle explored the great river all the way to its mouth at the Gulf of Mexico and claimed the entire Mississippi River valley in the name of France. Both of these parties, particularly that of La Salle, established contact with several Indian tribes along the course of the river, and La Salle actually visited a Natchez town—believed by some authorities to be Emerald Mound—and described it as a "beautiful eminence."

In 1699, Pierre le Moyne, sieur de d'Iberville, made a landfall along the Gulf Coast and reasserted France's claim to the Mississippi Valley. D'Iberville was responsible for the first trade contact with the Natchez tribe. By 1713, a trading post had been established at the Natchez capital on the site of modern Natchez. In 1716, the so-called "First Natchez War" resulted in the French strengthening their holdings in the area by the construction of Fort Rosalie, situated high above the Mississippi River on the grounds of the present-day Rosalie Mansion in downtown Natchez.

The Natchez people rebelled in November, 1729, and rose up against their French neighbors. Fort Rosalie was attacked, and the Indians killed 250 men and took 300 women and children as prisoners. The French immediately struck back and ruthlessly destroyed the Natchez nation for all time. The few members who survived the battle fled, only to be assimilated into other neighboring tribes. The white man's "influence" was dramatically and tragically felt by the Natchez Indians who were among the earliest to be decimated by European encroachment and interests.

A second disastrous French encounter with the Indians—this time, the Chickasaws—took place in 1736 near the Indian village of Ackia in the vicinity of today's Tupelo. Intent on reestablishing their superiority over the native people of the lower Mississippi valley after the Fort Rosalie massacre, as well as demanding the return of some of that uprising's Indian refugees who had joined the Chickasaw tribe, the French outfitted an expedition in New Orleans in February, 1736. Marching up the Mobile and Tombigbee Rivers, the 560-man army was joined by 600 Choctaws, the traditional enemies of the Chickasaw tribe.

Jean-Baptiste, sieur de Bienville, the brother of d'Iberville, led the expedition, and it was his plan to rendezvous with another French force led by Pierre d'Artaguette from the Indiana country. Arriving early, d'Artaguette's army attacked the Chickasaws immediately and was soundly defeated. When Bienville's troops arrived later, tired and short of supplies, they were so badly beaten in battle that they retreated all the way to Mobile.

The decisive defeat of d'Artaguette's and Bienville's armies proved to be the turning point of French influence in the Mississippi River valley. In addition to her American problems, France's fortunes in Europe were not faring too well during this period either. In 1762, as the result of the French and Indian War in America and the Seven Years' War on the Continent, France—in order to avoid relinquishing her North American possessions to the victorious British—ceded most of her holdings west of the Mississippi River to her ally, Spain. The following year, as dictated in the Treaty of Paris, England received France's possessions east of the Mississippi. The same treaty gave Spanish Florida to England in return for Havana, which had been seized by the British in the recent war. Britain immediately set to work to create a new colony from some of the land it acquired in the treaty. Fort Rosalie, at Natchez, was rebuilt and its name changed to Fort Panmure. The region became British West Florida, and it was held by the English for the next few years until the Spanish re-appeared on the Gulf Coast in 1779 and occupied Natchez in 1781.

British West Florida was very attractive to Americans living to the north and northeast, and during the British occupation there was a heavy influx of these primarily Scotch-Irish immigrants. The colony, even though populated in large part by native-born or adopted Americans, was intensely loyal to the British Crown during the Revolution, and did not figure prominently in the War.

The Second Treaty of Paris, signed in 1783 by England and the United States, ended the Revolutionary War, and also recognized the claim of the United States to West Florida, south all the way to the 31st parallel. The United States was only asserting its ownership to that part of the colony which was added to the original Spanish West Florida by the British after the First Treaty of Paris. Spain refused to accept the southern boundary as the extremity of the United States territory, and insisted instead that American claims stop at 32° 28' north parallel, or the northern boundary of the British-created colony. For several years the land between the two lines was in dispute. In 1795, Spain finally accepted the southern boundary as the legitimate one, but even then made no efforts to evacuate the region for three more years, or until the United States Congress organized the Mississippi Territory in 1798.

With the Spanish exit from the northern part of former British West Florida, all European power ended in the Natchez Trace region. Its southern portion had seen many masters: France, Britain, Spain, and finally, the infant United States. The multi-national influences would leave impressions on its land and its people for many years.

Hernando De Soto (circa 1500–1542), the Spanish explorer, was the first documented European to traverse much of the southeastern United States. His fortunes in the military service of Spain rose rapidly, and while still a young man, he accompanied and assisted Pizarro in his conquest of the Inca Empire in Peru. In 1539, De Soto and his followers landed in present-day Florida and began a three year exploration of today's states of Florida, Georgia, South Carolina, North Carolina, Tennessee, Alabama, Mississippi, Arkansas, Louisiana, and Texas. On March 4, 1541, the Chickasaws attacked de Soto's army and killed a dozen soldiers and destroyed fifty horses. A second attack on March 15 was repulsed by the Spaniards. On April 26, De Soto left the Chickasaw country once and for all—no doubt readily—after his disastrous encounter with the warlike tribe.

Drawing from Glazier's *Headwaters of the Mississippi*

De Soto Explorations. By the time De Soto and his men had discovered the Mississippi River in May, 1541, shown above, top, they had already established themselves as the first white men to encounter the Natchez Trace. The actual crossing of the Trace most likely took place just south of present-day Tu-pelo in the Chickasaw country near the spot where the Spanish party was attacked. A little over a year after his discovery of the Mississippi River, De Soto died, and his body was dropped into the mighty river somewhere in the vicinity of present-day Natchez (bottom).

Drawings from McGee's *History of Tennessee* [top] and Glazier's *Headwaters of the Mississippi* [Bottom]

Pierre le Moyne, sieur d'Iberville (1661–1706), was born in what is now Montreal. The son of a French colonist in Canada, he was one of several brothers who made an impact on the Gulf Coast area of America. D'Iberville reasserted France's claim to the Mississippi Valley by arriving there in 1699, only a few years after La Salle's explorations of the mighty river and its environs. He built Fort Maurepas on Biloxi Bay and established a post at Mobile.

Photograph courtesy of the Compte le Moyne de Martigny, Paris

Jean Baptiste, sieur de Bienville (1680–1768), was the younger brother of d'Iberville. Also born in Montreal, he accompanied his brother on his famous trip to the mouth of the Mississippi River. Bienville founded New Orleans in 1718 and made it the capital of French Louisiana in 1722. He served on and off as governor of the province until 1743, when he retired and returned to Paris.

Photograph courtesy of the Compte le Moyne de Martigny, Paris

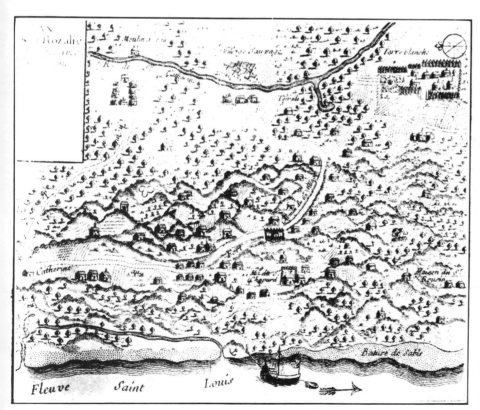

Fort Rosalie. This plan of Fort Rosalie and the neighboring Natchez villages originally appeared in Dumont de Montigny's *Memoires Historiques sur La Louisiane*, published in Paris in 1753. Fort Rosalie was built upon the bluffs overlooking the Mississippi River in 1716 and was named for the Duchess of Pontchartrain. According to Dumont, "it was merely a plot 25 fathoms long by 15 broad, inclosed with palisades, without any bastions. Inside, near the gate, was the guardhouse, and 3 fathoms off along the palisade ran the barracks for the soldiers. At the other end, opposite the gate, a cabin had been raised for the lodging of the officer on guard, and on the right of the entrance was the powder magazine.

Picture from Bulletin 43 of the Bureau of American Ethnology

Massacre at Fort Rosalie. Like all European newcomers to America, the French were quick to use a heavy hand in their dealings with the natives—in this case, the highly sophisticated Natchez tribe. In 1729, while at a meeting offering friendship to the unsuspecting French, the Indians rebelled against their overlords and massacred practically the entire garrison at Fort Rosalie. Only twenty white men and five Negroes escaped with their lives. This rather fanciful portrayal, painted many years after the incident, shows the fort high atop the bluffs, with the fighting Indians and Frenchmen shedding blood all around.

Photograph courtesy of the St. Louis Art Museum

D'Artaguette Monument. This monument, dedicated to the memory of Pierre d'Artaguette's stand against the Chickasaws in 1736, was erected in the vicinity of the battle by the Children of the American Revolution in 1934. D'Artaguette's army consisted of 145 Frenchmen and 326 Indians from Fort Chartres in the Illinois country. Short of supplies, the force struck the Chickasaws before Bienville's contingent could arrive. The monument tells the rest of the story.

Photograph courtesy of the United States National Park Service

Ackia Battleground National Monument. On October 25, 1938, a presidential proclamation established the Ackia Battleground National Monument three miles northwest of Tupelo, supposedly on the site of the Battle of Ackia. In later years this location was found to be inaccurate, and the town of Ackia was discovered to be within the Tupelo city limits. The National Monument was consequently dismantled in 1961 and its area was incorporated into the Natchez Trace Parkway and redesignated the Chickasaw Village Site. Shown here is one of the old national monument signs.

Photograph courtesy of the United States National Park Service

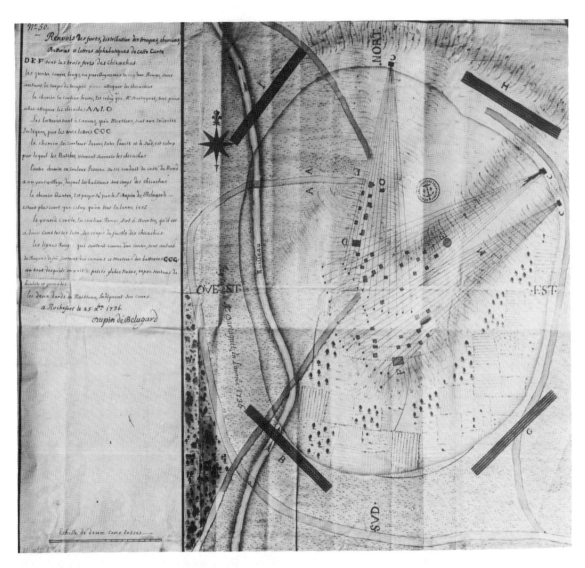

Ackia Battle Map. This ancient map, dated 1736, shows the French deployment of forces during the attack upon the Chickasaws at Ackia. Like d'Artaguette before him, Bienville rushed into an immediate attack on the numerically superior Chickasaws and was badly defeated. French influence in the region went from bad to worse after Ackia, until finally, after the French and Indian War, France withdrew from America forever, except for the brief time it held the Louisiana Territory at the beginning of the next century.

Photograph courtesy of the United States National Park Service

Manuel Luis Gayoso de Lemos y Amorin. In 1788, the Spanish authorities appointed Manuel Luis Gayoso de Lemos y Amorin (1752–1799) as governor with headquarters in Natchez. In 1789, on instructions from higher authority in New Orleans, Gayoso invited Americans to settle in the Natchez District, which was by rights already owned by the United States by virtue of the Second Treaty of Paris which it had signed with the British in 1783. Later married to an American woman, Gayoso spoke fluent English and got along very well with his American subjects.

Photograph courtesy of the Louisiana State Museum

Andrew Ellicott (1754–1820) was sent to Natchez in 1797 as the United States Commissioner with instructions to survey the 31st parallel which was the southern boundary of the Natchez District. For several years, the Spanish had been officially "off limits" at Natchez, since that part of Mississippi had been ceded to the United States by the British at the end of the Revolution. All during this time, Spain refused to accept the 31st parallel as the southern boundary of the United States claim. Finally, on March 30, 1798, Spanish troops evacuated Natchez and left the surrounding territory to its rightful owner, the United States. As Ellicott wrote in his journal regarding that momentous day, "I . . . walked to the fort, and found the last party, or rear guard just leaving it, and as the gate was left open, I went in, and enjoyed from the parapet, the pleasing prospects of the gallies and boats leaving the shore and getting underway. They were out of sight of the town before daylight."

Photograph reproduced from *The Dictionary of American Portraits*

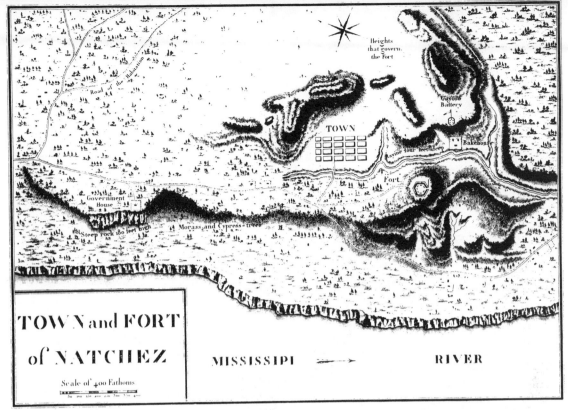

TOWN and FORT of NATCHEZ

MISSISSIPI ——→ RIVER

Scale of 400 Fathoms

Natchez, Mississippi. This map of Natchez, drawn just prior to the Spanish departure from the town, shows the old Spanish fort overlooking the Mississippi River. Much of the land shown lying between the village and the river has since been washed away by the Mississippi, and the road on the right side of the map—Silver Street—today fronts directly on the water.

Engraving by Georges H. V. Collot

Connelly's Tavern. When Andrew Ellicott appeared in Natchez in 1797 to settle once and for all the boundary between the American-held property ceded to the United States by the British at the end of the Revolution and that still claimed by Spain, he felt strongly enough that the town of Natchez belonged to the Americans that he raised the "Stars and Stripes" over Connelly's Tavern, where he was staying at the time. Actually, recent investigation has shown that Connelly's was not a tavern at all, but rather a private residence.

Photograph courtesy of Pelican Publishing Company

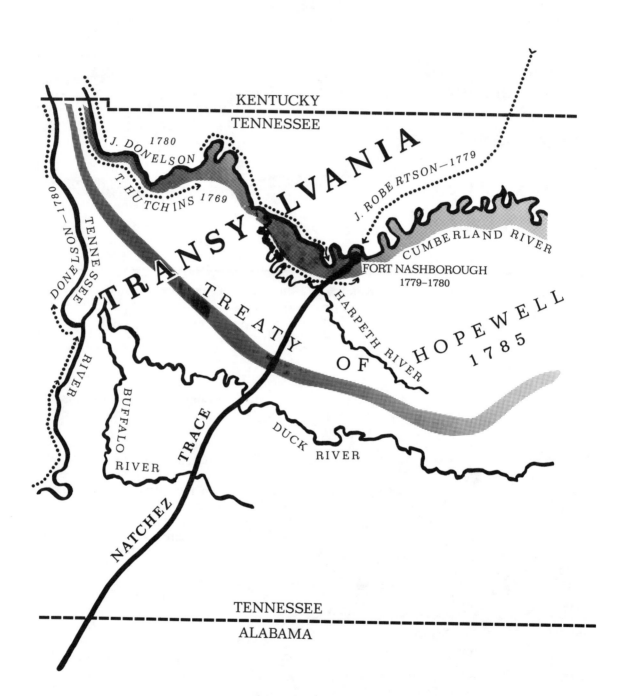

CHAPTER FIVE

American Settlement in the North

Natchez had been colonized under one flag or another for more than 150 years before the first permanent white settlers reached the Cumberland River valley at the northern end of the Natchez Trace. In fact, until the mid-eighteenth century, the entire region which later became Tennessee was a vast wilderness inhabited only by Indians and a few French trappers and traders. Slowly, however, settlement across the Appalachian Mountains started, and in 1768 Watauga, in what is now East Tennessee, was established. No sooner had the foothold across the mountains occurred than exploration began in the region even farther west.

The 1760s saw the appearance in Middle Tennessee of

Middle Tennessee. In Historic times the land encompassing present-day Middle Tennessee was claimed by the Cherokee tribe, although it maintained no villages in the region. In the early 1700s, a group of Shawnee Indians settled briefly on the site of Nashville, apparently in violation of an earlier agreement with the Cherokees. Sometime during this occupation by the Shawnees, a Frenchman, whose name has escaped history, and a boy by the name of Jean du Charleville established a trading post among the Indians. Thus the name "French Lick" was sometimes applied to the place where Nashville would one day be located. Around 1714, a joint Cherokee–Chickasaw war party drove the Shawnees from the region forever, and from then until the coming of the "Long Hunters," the Middle Tennessee landscape felt no footsteps except those of wandering Indians. The area was included in the colony of Transylvania in 1775, and after Richard Henderson lost most of his Kentucky land, he concentrated all of his efforts on the remainder of his real estate located in the great bend of the Cumberland. In 1783, James Robertson treatied with representatives from the Cherokee, Chickasaw, and Creek tribes at his station near Fort Nashborough. The cessions made by the Indians there were reaffirmed in 1785 at Hopewell, South Carolina, thereby officially freeing the land between the Cumberland River in the north and the Duck River in the south for settlement by the whites. During this time, all of the property in the present state of Tennessee was officially part of North Carolina and remained so until 1790, when it achieved territorial status and was called the Territory of the United States South of the River Ohio, or more commonly, the Southwest Territory.

Drawing by James A. Crutchfield and Edison Travelstead

bands of white pioneers, called "Long Hunters," who came through the wilderness from the eastern settlements to hunt and trap the virgin territory throughout the Cumberland valley. Their missions were temporary, however, and they were ever on the move as soon as they had finished hunting in one spot. It would take a different breed of men—and women—to move into the new territory with ax and plow and develop the countryside into farmland. During the 1770s, because of numerous reports by the hunters describing the rich land and great animal herds to be found in the Middle Tennessee region, many eastern settlers began to migrate westward to try their hands at the challenges presented by the new country.

In 1775, Richard Henderson traded the Cherokees out of several million acres of prime land in Kentucky and Middle Tennessee. He called his new land "Transylvania," and he organized a settlement party consisting of James Robertson and John Donelson who left separately from Fort Patrick Henry in Watauga for the west in late 1779. Robertson—traveling overland—arrived at the site of Nashville on December 25, 1779, while Donelson, aboard the flatboat "Adventure," followed the Tennessee, Ohio, and Cumberland rivers and disembarked on April 24, 1780. The place of settlement was on the banks of the Cumberland River, and the hastily constructed stockade was called Fort Nashborough, named after the North Carolina patriot Francis Nash.

The Indians made it clear from the very beginning that the white man's presence in their traditional hunting grounds was not welcome and would not be tolerated. Several forts, or stations, were built by the pioneers within a few miles of the main one at Nashborough in order to afford as much protection as possible from the Indians. A major attack on Freeland's Station in January, 1781, and another one on Fort Nashborough itself in April of the same year raised great fears among the newly arrived settlers, and many of them had serious doubts that they had done the right thing by migrating to the Cumberland country in the first place. A few pulled up stakes and either moved to the safety of Kentucky or back home.

By 1783, while Indian fears in Middle Tennessee continued, Natchez and the region surrounding it had passed from

British control to the United States. Most of the area, however, was still dominated by the Spanish, who refused to recognize the newly defined borders of the recently acquired American territory. Spain used its position to threaten United States' shipping on the Mississippi. Among those Americans most adversely affected were those living in the Cumberland settlements.

Of course, use of the Natchez Trace had already begun by this time, but for large and heavy produce, the overland route to Natchez, and to New Orleans beyond, was not practical. It made a lot more sense to float goods down the Cumberland, the Ohio, and the Mississippi rivers to their destinations, and to walk or ride back home, than to attempt to carry or haul tons of produce overland. In fact, carrying heavy goods overland was simply not possible, because the Trace at that time was still an unimproved forest path, where wagon or carriage travel was unthinkable.

Nashvillians had more important matters on their minds, however, than the ones concerning transportation of goods to market. The Indians were still acting up, and relief from their incessant forays was not in sight. As late as 1787, James Robertson was lamenting, ". . . I fear, without some timely assistance, we shall chiefly fall a sacrifice. . . ." Raids on outlying stations frequently caused the untimely death of their inhabitants. Finally, in 1792, at Buchanan's Station, the last great Indian battle was fought with the settlers, and peace was finally established on the Cumberland frontier.

There were bright spots in the early Nashvillians' lives, however. The town received its first merchant in 1783, and in 1784 Fort Nashborough officially became "Nashville." In 1785, the first school was established, and by 1787 the enterprising settlers had already built the Red Heifer Distillery where "whenever a run of the hot alcohol was ready, the custom was to blow a horn. At the sound of the horn all the thirsty souls hastened to the Red Heifer."

The school, the merchant, and the distillery notwithstanding, Nashville in the late 1780s was still just a wilderness outpost. A visitor of the times described it as ". . . a recently founded place" which contained "only two houses which; in true, merit that name; the rest are only huts that formerly served as a sort of fortification against Indian attacks. It is only about five years since the country began to develop; and, in the civilized portion of the Union, there are at present but few who know even its name." In 1787, there were only 477 white males over 21 years of age in the countryside surrounding Nashville. Negroes—male and female between the ages of 12 and 60—numbered 105. Taxes were being paid on 165,000 acres of land. A few years later, according to one historian, Nashville "was no longer in the open woods, but under fence; buffalo and deer did not race through the streets. Besides the six or eight log houses . . . there might be seen, in different directions among the cedars, ten or fifteen open shantees, and a few wagon and bark tents."

In 1788, a tall, lanky red-haired youth rode into Nashville with a satchel full of law books and little else. Unbeknown at the time, this immigrant would have a profound effect, not only on Nashville, on Tennessee, and on the United States, but his next few years in the region would be inextricably woven with the history of the Natchez Trace as well. Andrew Jackson was to travel the Trace often in the years to come—as merchant, as fiancé on the way to his marriage, and as commander of army troops. By the time he became president, the Trace's importance had already passed, but in the interval between his arrival in Nashville and his first administration, the old highway was to see more history in the making than almost any other section of comparable size in the country.

Timothy Demonbreun. The first claim by a white man to permanent settlement in the Nashville area goes to Jacques Timothe Boucher, sieur de Montbrun, or, as he has become known, Timothy Demonbreun (1747–1826). Born in Montreal, Demonbreun served in the French army in Canada during the French and Indian War. After his country was soundly defeated in the Battle of Quebec in 1759, he migrated south into what is now the United States and traded in furs with the Indians. Arriving at the future site of Nashville sometime during the 1760s, he took up residence in a cave high above the Cumberland River and was living there when the Robertson—Donelson parties arrived in 1779–1780. Afterwards, Demonbreun lived for a while in the stockade at Fort Nashborough, but later moved back outside where he lived for many years as one of Nashville's most respected citizens. No portrait of Demonbreun exists, but most likely, in his younger days, he looked much like this grizzled French trader and trapper.

Picture from *Pageant of America*

Long Hunter. During the 1760s and 1770s, several groups of men known collectively as the "Long Hunters" explored and hunted in the Middle Tennessee region. Gone from their homes sometimes for more than a year at a time, they would take their pelts and other products of their sojourns in the wilderness to market in Natchez. The hunters used the river system to get their products to Natchez, but it is undocumented as to how they got back to their homes in the Tennessee country. Judging from the manner that the later "Kaintucks" floated their wares downstream and then marched back overland along the Natchez Trace, it would seem reasonable that the "Long Hunters" did the same thing. If this is true, they may have been the first Americans to use the Natchez Trace as a thoroughfare for commerce, thus anticipating the "golden age" of the Trace by a score or so years.

Drawing from McGee's *History of Tennessee*

A Long Hunter

Thomas Hutchins' Log. Lieutenant Thomas Hutchins of the British Army was among the first white men to scientifically explore the Cumberland River valley. Hutchins' primary assignment was to patrol the western waters for French and Spanish traders who might be "Carrying on an illicit trade with our Indians. . . ." and "to prevent them from killing Buffalo. . . ." As a secondary mission, Hutchins surveyed and mapped great portions of the Cumberland and Tennessee rivers and kept a log describing his findings, a page of which is shown here. By 1769, he had reached the "French Lick," the future site of Nashville. Hutchins, in later years, became the "Geographer of the United States," a position which corresponded to today's Chief of the United States Army Corps of Engineers.

Photograph from Johnson's *Engineers on the Twin Rivers*

James Robertson. At the Treaty of Sycamore Shoals, in 1775, Richard Henderson, a North Carolina entrepreneur, purchased from the Cherokee Indians all of the land lying in the great bend of the Cumberland River in present-day Tennessee, as well as a large amount of real estate in Kentucky. Henderson christened the property "Transylvania," and he advertised for volunteers to go forth and settle the land (see illustration below). Henderson chose James Robertson and John Donelson, two of his friends and associates at Watauga, as his settlement party leaders. No likenesses exist today of either John Donelson (circa 1718–1786) or of Richard Henderson (1735–1785). This picture of James Robertson (1742–1814) portrays the man who would later earn the title "Father of Tennessee."

Picture from *Pageant of America*

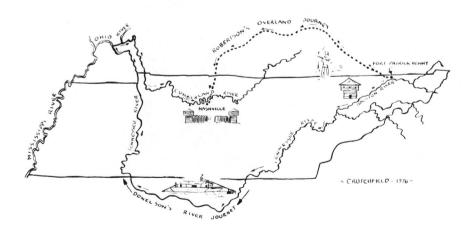

Robertson—Donelson Journeys. This map shows the routes taken by the Robertson–Donelson parties after their departure in 1779 from Fort Patrick Henry in the Watauga Settlements.

Drawing by James A. Crutchfield

Williamsburg Advertisement. This advertisement appeared in the *Virginia Gazette*, a Williamsburg newspaper, on September 30, 1775. Its purpose was to interest prospective settlers in the newly acquired lands west of the Appalachians. Colonel Richard Henderson, by virtue of his ownership of all the land along the Cumberland River, provided both the means and the impetus for the settlement of Nashville.

Picture from *Pageant of America*

Robertson's Cumberland River Crossing. With James Robertson as leader, the overland half of the settlement party left Watauga in November, 1779. With Robertson were the men and boys of the expedition, along with the livestock. Despite several hardships along the way, the party arrived at the site of Nashville on Christmas Day, 1779, and promptly crossed the Cumberland River on the ice. Locating on the south side of the river, along the line of bluffs which follow the stream for several miles, the men hastily reorganized themselves and built cabins and a stockade. This was Fort Nashborough, soon to become the nucleus of the Cumberland settlement experiement.

Painting by Sandor Bodo, courtesy of First Tennessee Bank, Nashville
Photograph by Henry Schofield Studios

Donelson's Arrival at Fort Nashborough. There was great joy at Nashborough when John Donelson's flotilla of boats was spotted coming around the last bend of the Cumberland River in the spring of 1780. Donelson's party had suffered a grueling voyage, hampered by severe weather, hostile Indians, and smallpox. Donelson wrote in his journal for April 24, 1780, "This day we arrived at our journey's end at the Big Salt Lick, where we have the pleasure of finding Capt. Robertson and his company.... Though our prospects at present are dreary, we have found a few log-cabins which have built on a cedar bluff above the Lick by Capt. Robertson and his company."

Painting by Sandor Bodo, courtesy of First Tennessee Bank, Nashville
Photograph by Henry Schofield Studios

Fort Nashborough was one of several stations built in the Cumberland River valley. Started by James Robertson's party in late 1779, Nashborough's population increased in April, 1780, when John Donelson, Robertson's partner in the movement from Watauga, arrived with the women and children. Before long several other forts, or stations as they were called, had sprung up all over the valley. Fort Nashborough, renamed Nashville in 1784, soon became pre-eminent on the western frontier.

Drawing from McGee's *History of Tennessee*

Defense of Fort Nashborough. Within a year after Nashborough was settled, it came very close to being destroyed. Indian hostilities had been an ever-present menace from the first day, but on April 1, 1781, an attack occurred so fierce and well-planned that, without the quick thinking of Mrs. Robertson, all might have been lost. The Indians lured a party of mounted men out of the fort, and immediately it was realized that an ambush was in progress. Charlotte Robertson, assessing the critical situation, released the dogs from the fortyard. The sudden appearance of these huge, growling, snarling canines frightened the Indians so badly that they quit the fight, thereby allowing the men time to retreat to the safety of the fort.

Drawing from McGee's *History of Tennessee*

Cumberland Valley Settler. It was not very long after the establishment of Fort Nashborough and the other stations throughout the Cumberland valley that some individuals tried to make a living outside the confines of the forts. In time this was practical, but during the first years of settlement it was extremely hazardous business. The region was thick with Indians, and the chances of making it on one's own without the support and protection of the rest of the settlement were slim indeed. On more than one occasion, after being tempted to leave the fort, a battered settler and his family would hastily return to its protection. Trials and tribulations were to visit the inhabitants of the Cumberland settlements many times before the region became totally safe for them and the thousands who followed. Finally, by the mid-1790s, most of the Indian troubles around Nashville had abated, and the forts and stations could be abandoned for the better life of the farms and towns.

Drawing from McGee's *History of Tennessee*

CHAPTER SIX

The Boatmen's Trail

It was only a matter of time until the fledgling settlements in the Cumberland River valley around Nashville had grown sufficiently in number and population to require a practical outlet for the produce of their farms. In addition to them, the settlements in Kentucky a few miles to the north around Boonesborough and Harrodsburg were expanding rapidly as well, and quite a sizable commerce had developed by the late 1780s. Year by year the volume of shipments increased until, by 1790, sixty-four boatloads of goods from Tennessee and Kentucky were processed at the market in Natchez.

New Orleans and Natchez were natural markets for the trans-mountain settlers of Tennessee and Kentucky to select to sell their goods. The only method of transporting wares to an alternative market back east was the overland route through hundreds of miles of untamed wilderness, or else overland as far as the Ohio River and then upriver to Pittsburgh and beyond. Neither of these choices was a good one, and each implied extensive planning, considerable time, and an abundance of labor. On the other hand, in order to move goods to Natchez or to New Orleans, all the farmer–merchant had to do was to build a flatboat, load it with his produce, and float it down the inland waterway system—the Ohio and Mississippi rivers, and in the case of the Nashvillians, the Cumberland—to market. Once there, after the goods had been sold, the flatboat was bro-

King's Tavern, located at the beginning of the Natchez Trace, is one of the oldest structures still standing in Natchez. The land and building were granted to Prosper King by the Spanish authorities in 1789, and from that date until 1820 the property was operated as a tavern. The long journey up the Natchez Trace, with the dangers of outlaws, often led travelers to group together for protection, and King's Tavern was used as a gathering place for these individuals and parties ready to make the trip. The first United States mail ever delivered from Nashville to Natchez was first brought to King's Tavern for distribution to the town's citizens.

Photograph courtesy of the United States National Park Service

ken up, sold for lumber, and the owner and his crew walked back home along the old Indian trail which would later become known as the Natchez Trace.

These simple business transactions by Tennessee and Kentucky backwoodsmen were responsible for the genesis of an entire era of life and lore along the Natchez Trace. The period has become known as the "Boatmen's Era," because during its brief life from the early and middle 1780s to around 1811, thousands and thousands of farmers-turned-boatmen shipped millions of pounds of farm produce and home industry products down the Mississippi, sold their goods, collected their money, and made their way back up the Natchez Trace to Nashville, and to their respective homes.

Now it is only reasonable to assume that, on the wild fringes of civilization, separated from the sophisticated eastern cities by hundreds of miles of wilderness and months of travel, there would exist temptations designed by evil men to encourage a recently paid backwoodsman to spend his money. At Natchez, this temptation came in the form of a small area of businesses situated along the banks of the Mississippi River and called Natchez "under the hill." Liquor and wild women abounded here, and just about anything one might imagine could be had for the asking—and the paying. Many an innocent "Kaintuck"—as the flatboatmen were collectively called, whether or not they came from Kentucky—walked away from one of these brothels with nothing more to show for his months of hard labor than the clothes he was wearing.

While Natchez "under the hill" flourished, a more proper neighborhood had developed at Natchez "on the hill," the high bluff which overlooked the Mississippi River and its "riff-raff" below. But the "Kaintucks" and their kinsmen had little business in this section of the Spanish–American town, and except for passing through it to get to the Natchez Trace in order to start their long trips back home, most missed the amenities of this other side of Natchez society.

For the boatmen who had escaped the clutches of the wenches and the flow of the booze at the "under the hill" dives, there now was the 450-mile journey through the wilderness.

There were few accommodations of any type from Bayou Pierre, a few miles out of Natchez, all the way to Nashville. In the later years of the Trace's development, inns, or stands, grew up along its route to offer food and lodging to the weary traveler. But, during the "boatmen's" era, the best one could hope for was pitching camp right beside the Trace and sleeping under the stars, or else, perhaps spending the night with one of the few farmers who lived along the way.

If the after-effects of Natchez "under the hill" and the lack of accommodations along the Natchez Trace on the homeward journey were not enough to trouble the tired "Kaintucks," then there was one more element of the trip which was more foreboding than either of the other two. That fear was the rapidly growing contingent of highwaymen who frequented the Trace.

During the early years of American travel along the Natchez Trace, the entire section represented the leading edge of pioneer settlement in this part of the United States. Realizing this, and considering the fact that there was a growing abundance of monied travelers using the Trace, it becomes understandable why the thoroughfare attracted large numbers of the lawless who survived by lifting the pocketbooks from boatmen and other wayfarers.

The most notorious outlaw band to frequent the Natchez Trace and the surrounding area was the one led by the Harpe brothers. Operating at an early date out of East Tennessee, Micajah and Wiley—called Big and Little Harpe respectively—caused such havoc with their misdeeds there that they eventually gravitated to the wilderness realms of Middle Tennessee, Kentucky, and the Natchez Trace. The Harpes can only be described as psychotic killers who had no regard for human life or property. Many victims were claimed by the brothers, including Micajah's own child, whom, during a fit of anger, Big Harpe took by the heels and smashed into a tree!

With the likes of the Harpe brothers for a starter, the Natchez Trace rapidly became a gathering place for the criminal element of southern America. While the number of outlaws who patroled the Trace's length did not reach the proportions that it did during the later period of the road's history, the

Harpes and others like them were the first in a long line of notorious criminals who made their headquarters in the forests between Natchez and Nashville.

The time of the "boatmen's" trail in Natchez Trace history overlapped to a certain extent that of the next period when the United States aspired to convert the old trail into a national road. At the turn of the eighteenth century, while the Government was laying plans for the acquisition of the property from the Indians and making decisions for the improvement of the Natchez Trace, the road was still used day in and day out by "Kaintucks" and others just as it had been all through the 1780s and 1790s. In fact, the boatmen used the trail for several years after the improvements were made, since it was still the only practical way to get to Tennessee, Kentucky, and points beyond from Natchez and New Orleans. Not until the advent and proliferation of the steamboat were the commercial uses of the Natchez Trace replaced by the more universal ones of mail service, transportation of military troops, and private travel in general.

Life on a Flatboat. Since the "Kaintucks" necessarily lived aboard their crafts for weeks at a time, some of the more elaborate ones were fitted out with sleeping quarters and a fireplace, upon which to cook and for heat in cold weather. But none of the boats were so valuable that they could not be broken up into lumber at their destination, and for good reason. It took thirty men a total of three months to row and pole a flatboat from New Orleans to Cairo, in the Illinois country. On the other hand, the time required to walk the Trace to Nashville, and then to travel one of the northern roads out of that town to the same destination, was far shorter—and easier.

Drawing from *Pageant of America*

Flatboat. The "boatmen's," or "flatboat" era of the Natchez Trace began when Kentuckians and Tennesseans discovered that it was relatively simple to float their produce downstream from their homes to Natchez and New Orleans. The return trip was made by setting out on foot along the old Indian trail connecting Natchez and Nashville, which was later called the Natchez Trace. While hiking through the wilderness was a tough assignment, it was not as difficult as rowing and poling a heavy flatboat back home *upstream* for more than 1000 miles.

Drawing from *Pageant of America*

Cordelling Upstream. The alternative to walking back along the Natchez Trace was poling, rowing, and "cordelling" a flatboat or keelboat back upstream. Cordelling consisted of the crew walking up the bank of the river, literally pulling the craft by a rope attached to it. Understandably, most of the "Kaintucks" chose to walk home from their missions in Natchez and New Orleans rather than take part in this back-breaking labor.

Drawing by James A. Crutchfield from Johnson's *Engineers on the Twin Rivers*

The "Kaintucks." To the people along the lower Mississippi, the flatboatmen eventually became known as "Kaintucks," whether or not they hailed from Kentucky. Even though the "Kaintucks" started out as farmers-turned-boatmen, in time a professional class of flatboatmen evolved, who made it their business to haul goods downstream to Natchez and New Orleans. A contemporary observer was not too kind in his remarks of the group as a whole. According to him, the "Kaintucks" were ". . . dirty as Hottentots, their dress a shirt and trousers of canvass, black, greasy, and sometimes in tatters, the skin burnt wherever exposed to the sun, each with a budget, wrapt up in an old blanket, their beards eighteen days old, added to the singularity of their appearance, which was altogether savage."

Drawing courtesy of the Tennessee Historical Society

King's Tavern. In this modern drawing, King's Tavern shows its original structural lines. Built of brick, heavy timbers fitted together with pegs, cypress clapboards, and poplar wood, the soundly constructed, three-story house is today used just as it was originally—as a tavern and restaurant.

Drawing by Carol (Crook) Levy

New Orleans Wharf. The final desination for many of the Kentucky and Tennessee flatboats was Natchez. Many others, however, went to the larger and more profitable market at New Orleans farther down the Mississippi River. This drawing of the wharf at New Orleans shows quite dramatically the great number of flatboats of every description pulled up to its docks. What had started out as a small operation in the 1780s, with a few boats going downstream to market, had turned into big business by 1800. An 1801 Nashville newspaper claimed that over $120,000 had passed through its town in payment for produce shipped downriver from Tennessee, Kentucky, and points east.

Picture from *Pageant of America*

PRICES CURRENT,

NATCHEZ, AUGUST, 10, 1802.
Bacon, per lb. 10 to 12½ cents, brisk
Bar Iron, per cwt. 16 dollars.
Castings, small, per do 10 dollars.
Cordage, per cwt 12½ to 15 dollars
Corn, per bushel 50 cents very dull.
Corn, meal per bbl. 3 dolls. dull.
Flour, per bbl. 4 dolls. dull.
Lime, per bushel 25 to 37½ cents, great quantities at market.
Peach brandy, per gallon, 1 dollar.
Whisky, per do 75 to 100 cents, scarce
Pork, salted, per bbl 10 dollars.
Tobacco, per cwt. 3 to 3½ dolls. dull.
Walnut and cherry plank, per 100 feet 4 dollars;

———

NEW-ORLEANS.

Cotton, per cwt. 18 to 20 dols.
Flour, per bbl. 4 to 5 dols.
Tobacco, per cwt. 3 1-2 to 4 dols.
Bacon per cwt. 15 dols.
Sugar, brown, per cwt. 7 dols.
Logwood, per cwt. 28 dols.
Iron, bar, per cwt. 10 dollars.

☞ *Advertisements, &c. omitted for want of room, will be inserted in an extra paper to-morrow.*

Natchez Advertisement. An advertisement from the Natchez newspaper, *Mississippi Herald*, dated August 10, 1802, gives prices of commodities in both Natchez and New Orleans. Such prices made it profitable for a backwoodsman in Kentucky or Tennessee to ship his produce downstream to either of the two towns, where he received considerably more for them than he could at home.

Picture from *Pageant of America*

Natchez, Mississippi was the leading town in what is now Mississippi during the days of the flatboatmen. It had grown considerably since the days when it consisted of only Fort Rosalie and a few houses scattered here and there. The entire Mississippi Territory, when it was organized in 1798, contained around 5000 people, the majority of whom lived in the Natchez District. Because of its premier standing in the region, Natchez was chosen as the first territorial capital, a position it maintained until the seat of government was removed to Washington in 1802. By the time this engraving was made in the late 1790s, Natchez was a good sized town. The road to the right of the Spanish fort descended to the Mississippi River, and it was down this street that the infamous "under the hill" bars and brothels did their "evil" business. One contemporary visitor, who spent thirty days in

this area, declared, ". . . it would be my delight to give you a description of some of the scenes that came under my observation during this period, but am restrained by the conscientious fact that the refined could not, would not tolerate them, when you came to lay them before the public."

Engraving by Georges H. V. Collot

Silver Street. Over the years, much of the original Natchez "under the hill" neighborhood has been washed away by the Mississippi River. Today, the only reminder of this once notorious section, which in its time witnessed murders, robberies, thuggings, prostitution, and every other kind of malice, is Silver Street, presently being structually restored and converted into an avenue of shopping facilities. This photo shows Silver Street as it appeared about thirty years ago.

Photograph courtesy of the United States National Park Service

Winthrop Sargent (1753–1820) was the first governor of the Mississippi Territory, and it was he who first called on the United States government to improve the Natchez Trace. In September, 1798, immediately after his appointment to the governorship, Sargent wrote to the United States secretary of state, Timothy Pickering, suggesting the construction of a post road from Nashville to Natchez. Not long afterwards, on the second Monday in January, 1800, mail service between the two towns was established, using the Natchez Trace as its route.

Photograph reproduced from *The Dictionary of American Portraits*

William Charles Cole Claiborne (1775–1817) was a Virginia native living in Nashville when President Thomas Jefferson called on him to become the second governor of the Mississippi Territory. Claiborne had already served on the Tennessee Superior Court from 1796 until 1797, and had succeeded Andrew Jackson to the United States House of Representatives. His first act was to move the capital of the Territory from Natchez to Washington. When his term was over, the affairs of the Territory were in much better condition than they were before.

Photograph from *Pageant of America*

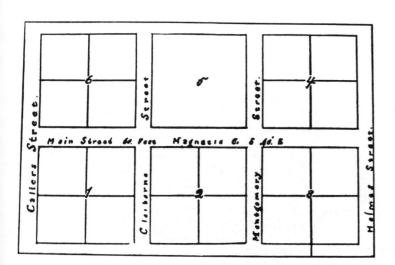

Washington, Mississippi. The second governor of the Mississippi Territory, W.C.C. Claiborne, was responsible for moving the capital about six miles up the Natchez Trace from Natchez to Washington. Washington was a new town, just established, and Claiborne's son, years later, wrote of it, "It was a gay and fashionable place, compactly built for a mile or more from east to west, every hill in the neighborhood occupied by some gentleman's chateau. . . . It was, of course, the haunt of politicians and office hunters; the center of political intrigue; the point to which all persons in the pursuit of land or occupation first came. It was famous for its wine parties and its dinners, not unfrequently enlivened by one or more duels directly afterward."

Picture from *Pageant of America*

Mount Locust. About a day's walk on the Natchez Trace from Natchez was Mount Locust, a home belonging to William Ferguson. Whether he wanted to or not, Ferguson soon found himself opening the doors of his home to wayfarers on their way to Nashville. In later years, Ferguson developed Mount Locust into a full-fledged stand, or inn, but in the early days it was his generosity and not his business which reached out to the tired "Kaintucks" as they reached his home at the end of the first day's journey out of Natchez.

Drawing from *Mount Locust on the Old Natchez Trace*

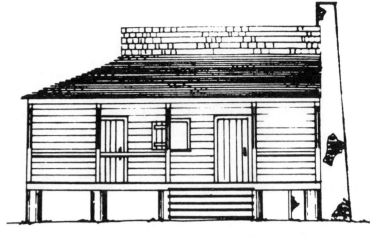

Mount Locust and Union Town. Ferguson and four friends and neighbors decided that with the Natchez Trace developing into a major thoroughfare between Natchez and Nashville, they should organize a township at Mount Locust and cash in on the commerce in the region. The town was mapped out, and lots were put on the market for sale. Several businessmen, including a doctor, a tanner, a storekeeper, a brick maker, a cabinet maker, and the owner of a cotton gin, operated in the village, called Union Town. Ferguson had ambitions for his town to be named county seat, but when it was passed over for the honors, it finally declined, leaving only Mount Locust to develop into a first class hostelry.

Drawing from *Mount Locust on the Old Natchez Trace*

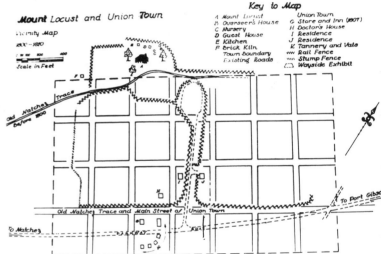

Natchez Advertisement. This advertisement in the *Mississippi Herald and Natchez Gazette* on October 21, 1807, touted the services of a "Z. Mangrum's House of Entertainment." Shortly afterward Union Town became deserted, having lost its race with a neighboring town for the county seat.

Picture from *Mount Locust on the Old Natchez Trace*

THE subscriber informs his friends and the public that he has opened a *House of Entertainment,* At Union Town, in the House formerly occupied as a Store-House by Ferguson & Woolley, where he has on hand, and will constantly keep, a full and general supply of necessaries for the accommodation of travellers :—he is provided with good Stables and provender for horses—and hopes by his attention to the business, to merit a share of the public patronage.

Z. MANGUM.

Union Town, October 15.   42—3

Andrew Jackson (1767–1845) established several business connections in Natchez shortly after he arrived in Nashville. In fact, Jackson became so involved with the merchants of Natchez that he acquired some land at Bayou Pierre, north of town, and built a cabin. In 1791, Jackson made one of his most memorable trips down the Natchez Trace from Nashville to meet his fiancée, Rachel Donelson Robards.

Drawing by Jim Farrell from Crutchfield's *Footprints Across the Pages of Tennessee History*

Rachel Jackson (1767–1828) was the daughter of Nashville's co-founder, John Donelson. An unhappy marriage at a young age to Lewis Robards of Kentucky finally produced a separation and drove Rachel to Natchez to escape her husband's rumored visit to Nashville. While Rachel was in Natchez, word reached Nashville and Andrew Jackson that a divorce had been granted to the Robards. Jackson immediately headed off down the Natchez Trace to Rachel.

Drawing by Jim Farrell from Crutchfield's *Footprints across the Pages of Tennessee History*

Francis Baily (1774–1844), an Englishman who in later life became a founder and four-times president of the Royal Astronomical Society of Great Britain, traveled over the Natchez Trace in 1797 from Natchez to Nashville. His vivid account of the trip, as a typical traveler of the times, has done much to shed light on the primitive road conditions of the day and of the inconveniences and dangers which were constant companions of the early wayfarer.

Reproduction of oil painting in the Royal Astronomical Society, London

The Springfield Plantation, just north of Natchez on the Natchez Trace, was owned by Thomas Green, a friend of Rachel Donelson's family. This was the place to which Rachel had fled in order to avoid an unpleasant confrontation with her estranged husband in Nashville. When Andrew Jackson heard of the divorce of the Robards, he quickly journeyed to Springfield where he and Rachel were married in the summer of 1791.

Photograph courtesy of the United States National Park Service

JOURNAL

OF A

TOUR IN UNSETTLED PARTS

OF

NORTH AMERICA

IN 1796 & 1797.

BY THE LATE

FRANCIS BAILY, F.R.S.,

PRESIDENT OF THE ROYAL ASTRONOMICAL SOCIETY.

With a Memoir of the Author.

LONDON:

BAILY BROTHERS, ROYAL EXCHANGE BUILDINGS.

MDCCCLVI.

Baily's *Journal*. A book describing Francis Baily's visit to the United States was published posthumously in 1856. Entitled *Journal of a Tour in Unsettled Parts of North American in 1796 and 1797*, its detailed passages regarding the Englishman's trip along the Natchez Trace in 1797 are especially interesting in their descriptions of early travel conditions.

Title page of original edition from the 1969 reprint by Southern Illinois University Press

Bayou Pierre. Francis Baily accurately described Bayou Pierre as "a little stream which rises up in the district of Natchez; and upon the headwaters of which, there are some settlements which form part of that district. . . ." On his journey up the Natchez Trace, Baily said, "This place . . . is the most northern frontier settlement in the district. From this place, then, we have to date our departure into the wilderness; and here we have to bid adieu to all marks of civilization till we arrive at the borders of the Cumberland River, in the State of Tennessee, a distance of about six hundred miles. . . ."

Photograph courtesy of the United States National Park Service

Log House along the Trace. During the early "flatboat" days, there were few if any at all, inns in which the "Kaintucks" and other travelers could stay. Here and there, in the stretch of wilderness between Bayou Pierre and the outskirts of Nashville, there were a few cabins owned by individuals intent on making their living from the soil and the forests. Normally, these homeowners would open their doors to travelers, and in some cases, the increased traffic proved to be so lucrative that a few converted their houses into hostelries. The picture shows an old engraving of a typical log house in the wilderness along the Natchez Trace.
Picture from *Pageant of America*

"Kaintucks" Break Camp. For years during the "boatmen's" era, the traveling "Kaintucks" had no place to spend the night other than on the trail. The proliferation of inns and stands did not materialize until several years later, and the only alternatives open to a flatboatman in the way of accommodations was to talk a farmer into letting him spend the night at his house or simply sleeping outdoors along the Trace. Most times, several returning boatmen would group together and travel up the Trace in a party for protection. This old engraving shows a group of "Kaintucks" breaking camp in anticipation of a long day's journey ahead.
Engraving reproduced from *The American Revolution—A Picture Sourcebook*

Hanging by the Neck. While the outlaws and highwaymen along the Natchez Trace were not as prolific during the late 1790s as they became in the early 1800s, they were still a nuisance. The law finally caught up with Little Harpe, the infamous younger member of the notorious Harpe brother gang, and on February 8, 1804, he was ordered to be "hung up by the neck, between the hours of ten o'clock in the forenoon and four in the afternoon, until he is dead, dead, dead." The site of the hanging was along the Natchez Trace at the old town of Greenville, in Jefferson County, Mississippi, located about twenty miles northeast of Natchez.
Engraving reproduced from *The American Revolution—A Picture Sourcebook*

Settlers along the Trace. Although the Natchez Trace was used primarily as a return route to Nashville by the boatmen and for other travelers during this period, the thoroughfare was used occasionally by immigrants seeking a new life to the south. In 1789, the Spanish governor-general at New Orleans invited Americans to settle in the Natchez area. This proposal accounted for some increased north–south traffic. However, when the Mississippi Territory was created in 1798, a flood of Americans rushed into the area, intent on grabbing up the valuable land and beginning their lives anew. This scene shows a party of settlers headed south along the Natchez Trace.

Picture courtesy of the Federal Highway Administration

Metal Ford. Bridges were a convenience of the future when the first "Kaintucks" hiked the Natchez Trace. Rivers and streams that were shallow enough were crossed at fords, like the one called Metal Ford on the Buffalo River in Tennessee. Sometimes, during the rainy season, the waters of the rivers were so great that the men could not attempt to cross them for fear of losing their horses and equipment. This photo shows Metal Ford as it appears today. The ford derived its name from the hardpan rock—like metal—which underlined the Buffalo River at this particular place.

Photograph courtesy of the United States National Park Service

Jack's Branch. As the "Kain-tucks" made their way up the Natchez Trace into Tennessee, the old trail looked much like this modern-day segment at Jack's Branch, about seventy miles south of Nashville. Today the National Park Service has provided a picnic area and rest-rooms along this picturesque section of the Natchez Trace Parkway.

Photograph courtesy of the United States National Park Service

Cabin along the Trace. When Francis Baily and his companions finally approached Nashville, after their long and arduous trip up the Natchez Trace, they were delighted to see, in a clearing, a house and farm belonging to a man by the name of Jocelyn. Here, Baily and his friends were treated to their first decent meal since leaving Natchez—boiled bacon, French beans, and corn bread. Baily described Jocelyn's farm as consisting of "several acres of land tolerably well cultivated; some in corn, some in meadow, and others in grain." Jocelyn's house was a two-room log affair, and most likely looked a great deal like this cabin, which still stands nearby today, and which itself was a stopping place on the Natchez Trace.

Photograph courtesy of the United States National Park Service

Francois Andre Michaux (1770–1855) was a French naturalist who was commissioned by his government to explore the interior parts of the United States to locate specimens of plants which would grow in and be of benefit to his native country. In late August, 1802, Michaux's journey carried him to Nashville. He found the young town on the northern end of the Natchez Trace to contain about 130 houses of which only eight were built of brick. Of the business climate, Michaux declared, "This little town, although built upwards of fifteen years, contains no kind of manufactory or public establishment; but there is a printing-office which publishes a newspaper once a week. They have also began to found a college . . . but this establishment was only in its infancy, having but seven or eight students and one professor."

Picture from Thwaites' *Early Western Travels*

Michaux's Travels. Michaux published the diary of his journey to America as soon as he returned to France. The book went through several editions in French and English, and was extremely popular on the continent because of its vivid descriptions of the United States and the lifestyles of its inhabitants. Michaux was aware of the value of the Natchez Trace to the Tennessee and Kentucky communities, commenting, "All the inhabitants of the western country who go by the river to New Orleans, return by land, pass through Nashville [sic], which is the first town beyond the Natches [sic]. The interval that separates them is about six hundred miles, and entirely uninhabited; which obliges them to carry their provisions on horseback to supply them on the road." Elsewhere in his book, Michaux explained, "The road that leads to the Natches [sic] was only a path that serpentined through these boundless forests, but the federal government have just opened a road, which is on the point of being finished, and will be one of the finest in the United States. . . ."

Title page of original edition reproduced from Thwaites' *Early Western Travels*

TRAVELS

TO THE WEST OF THE

ALLEGHANY MOUNTAINS,

IN THE STATES OF

Ohio,

KENTUCKY, AND TENNESSEA,

AND BACK TO CHARLESTON, BY THE UPPER CAROLINES;

COMPRISING

The most interesting Details on the present State of

Agriculture,

AND

THE NATURAL PRODUCE OF THOSE COUNTRIES:

TOGETHER WITH

Particulars relative to the Commerce that exists between the above-mentioned States, and those situated East of the Mountains and Low Louisiana,

UNDERTAKEN, IN THE YEAR 1802,

UNDER THE AUSPICES OF

His Excellency M. CHAPTAL, Minister of the Interior,

BY F. A. MICHAUX,

MEMBER OF THE SOCIETY OF NATURAL HISTORY AT PARIS; CORRESPONDENT OF THE AGRICULTURAL SOCIETY IN THE DEPARTMENT OF THE SEINE AND OISE.

London:

Printed by D. N. SHURY, Berwick Street, Soho.

FOR B. CROSBY AND CO. STATIONERS' COURT;

AND J. P. HUGHES, WIGMORE STREET, CAVENDISH SQUARE.

1805.

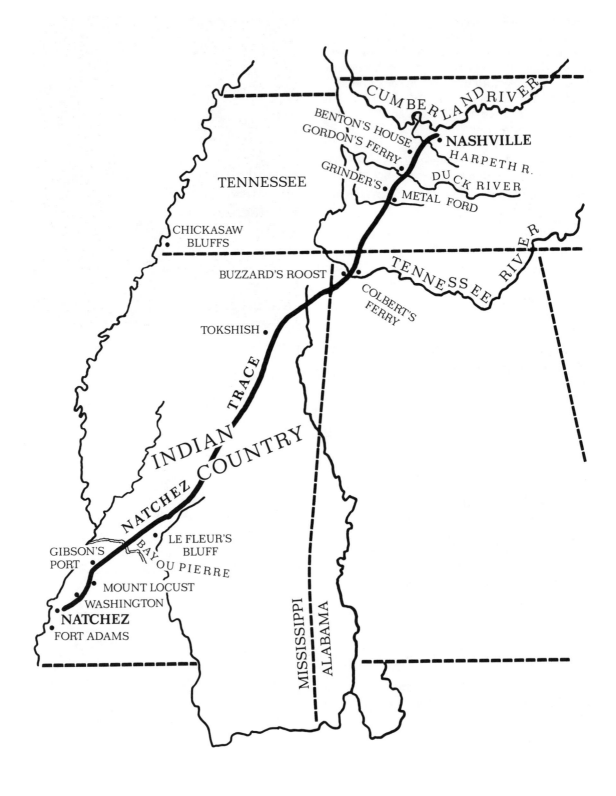

CHAPTER SEVEN

A National Road

The beginning of the nineteenth century brought with it a new dimension to the history and utility of the Natchez Trace. With the establishment of the Mississippi Territory in 1798, it became necessary for the Union to maintain some sort of communications with this outpost of civilization, separated as it was from Tennessee and points north by miles of Indian territory. In those days, the middle and northern sections of today's State of Mississippi still belonged to the Choctaws and the Chickasaws, and it was not until several years later, when treaties with these tribes turned those sections over to the United States, that private citizens were allowed to homestead in them.

As early as 1798, the very year of the territory's organization, its first governor, Winthrop Sargent, brought to the attention of the central government in Washington the fact that communications—particularly United States mail facilities—were sorely lacking in the region, and that the problem should be addressed immediately. Accordingly, mail service was initiated between Nashville and Natchez on the Natchez Trace a

---

The Trace in Early 1800s. During its last phase of popularity as a leading road in the old Southwest, the Natchez Trace had a totally different appearance than it did in the early days of its development. The 1801 treaties with the Chickasaws and the Choctaws allowed the Federal government the right to improve the road, but they specifically prohibited the opening of inns or other travel accommodations. It was not long, however, before that aspect of the agreements was broken, and many stands opened up all along the route, each providing food and lodging of varying quality to weary travelers. Ferries were built to assist wayfarers across the wider rivers, and swamps and marshes, which heretofore had to be walked around or through, were bridged with causeways, thus allowing one to cross dryshod. In order to accommodate the needs of outlying villages, the northern end of the Trace, from about thirty miles south of Nashville, took several routes into the town on the banks of the Cumberland River. Consequently, today, there is no one route from the Natchez Trace leading into Nashville. Over the years, the subject has been hotly debated as to just where the "real" Natchez Trace's route passed.

Drawing by James A. Crutchfield and Edison Travelstead

short time later. The Trace was in such a primitive condition, however, that it did not take long for the authorities in both Natchez and Washington to agree on the need for its improvement.

In March, 1801, the postmaster-general of the United States wrote to the Secretary of War suggesting that the mail service was difficult and expensive to maintain "on account of the badness of the road which is said to be no other than an Indian footpath very devious & narrow." The postmaster-general suggested that United States Army troops be employed in an improvement effort, since there were "a considerable number of troops . . . stationed in that part of the country & it being also a time of peace, it struck me that their services could not be turned to more advantage than by employing them in clearing out a waggon-road & in bridging the creeks & causewaying the swamps between Nashville and Natchez."

Treaties in late 1801 with the Chickasaws at Chickasaw Bluffs and with the Choctaws at Fort Adams, south of Natchez, provided the government with the authority to work on the Natchez Trace. Immediately afterwards, the construction work was begun. The ink had hardly dried on the treaty papers before the army troops began clearing underbrush and building bridges. Their efforts must have progressed rather rapidly at first, for a letter, dated January, 1802, just a few weeks after the completion of the Indian treaties in October and December of the previous year and written from the army garrison on the Tennessee River indicated that "we have nothing new to relate from this place—the troops are at present upon the road, & we expect to reach Duck River in a few weeks."

A year later, Colonel Thomas Butler, the army officer overseeing the work on the northern end of the Trace, was transferred to Fort Adams. Even by then, however, there was still a great deal of work to be done. "On the subject of the road-cutting business permit me to recommend a regular succession of parties of thirty men each, to be relieved once a month, and that the road be opened not exceeding sixteen feet in width and not more than eight feet of the sixteen to be cut close to the ground, and smoothed for passengers," the Secretary of War wrote in February, 1803. He added that, "The great object is to have a comfortable road for horses and foot passengers, and instead of the expense of cutting a wide road, it is much more important that the swamps and streams should be causewayed & bridged."

By the time the work was discontinued in late 1803, about 264 miles of the Trace's approximate 450 mile length had been improved. The *Natchez Trace Survey*, published in 1941, concluded that the reason for the job's lack of completion was that the task had been entirely too large for the United States Army to undertake in the first place, and that "to call on it for constructing so extensive a job as building the Natchez Trace was to expect too much."

With the improvements along the Trace, and the increased traffic which those improvements brought, there grew an even more important need for lodging and eating facilities along its route. During the earlier years crude arrangements were satisfactory for the rough and tough "Kaintucks," but since the Natchez Trace was now taking on a different character—that of a "national" road and therefore, attracting travelers from all walks of life—other alternatives had to be considered. Inns, or stands as they were called, were gradually established every few miles along the Trace's length. A weary traveler could obtain a couple of hot meals and in most cases spend the night more comfortably than he could on the hard ground.

In the meantime, the outlaws along the Natchez Trace during this period had become even more numerous than they had been in the days of the "Kaintucks" and flatboatmen. Tennessee's governor Archibald Roane, writing of his concern to the United States Secretary of War in 1803, stated that "The road passing through the Indian Country from Nashville to Natchez has for some time past been infested with a gange of Bantitti [sic], whether White men or Indians, or both, has not been fully ascertained." The Secretary of War replied that the problem was of the gravest concern in Washington, and that "The President of the United States is desirous of affording every aid in his power for rendering the intercourse between Tennessee and Natchez as safe and convenient as circumstances will permit." Army troops were stationed at the Tennessee and Duck rivers for the "express purpose of giving all the protection to travelers in our power." Additionally, the President offered "a reward of four hundred dollars to any Citizen or Indian who shall apprehend one or more of the Banditti who have been guilty of attacking, robing & murdering persons on the road to the Indian Country between Nashville and Natchez. . . ."

Beginning in 1806, additional efforts were made to improve the Natchez Trace. On April 21 of that year, the Post Office Department had a $6000 appropriation "to cause to be opened a road from Nashville in the State of Tennessee, to Natchez, in the Mississippi Territory." Bids were let for these improvements with the stipulation that the road be completed by October 1, 1807. Total expenses for the project were not to exceed $5,400. The road was to be cleared to a width of twelve feet, with no stumps left standing higher than sixteen inches above the ground. For the covenience and safety of the post rider, the center four feet of the path was to be cleared all the way to the ground. These improvements had doubtful results, raising questions from a few of those in authority at the time of whether the road was in any better shape after improvement than it was before.

Monies for the Natchez Trace's modernization came slowly over the next few years. In fact, during the entire twenty years of so-called improvement, only $22,000 was spent altogether. By the end of that period, however, the old trail had just about lost its importance anyway, and travelers were using more direct and convenient routes for passage between Nashville and Natchez.

Army Troops Improving the Trace. It was in early 1801 that the postmaster-general of the United States suggested employing United States Army troops to assist in the improvement of the Natchez Trace. In his letter to the secretary of war, he stated, "It is no novel thing I believe to employ the military in clearing & in making causeways and bridges even in our own country: I believe it was frequently done during the late war. Moderate labour it is believed would tend no less to preserve the health & activity than the morals of the troops." Troops were thereafter assigned for this task, and while awaiting treaty meetings which the Chickasaws and the Choctaws which occurred later in the year, the secretary of war suggested that the Army get started on the Tennessee end of the Trace in Davidson and Williamson counties, since that part was within the jurisdiction of the state.

Drawing from *The American Revolution—A Picture Sourcebook*

Edmund Pendleton Gaines (1777–1849) was a first lieutenant in the United States Army when he assisted in the surveying of the Natchez Trace in anticipation of the government improvement program. Gaines, a few years later assisted in the arrest of Aaron Burr, who was wanted by federal authorities on treason charges, and who was active in the Natchez Trace region. Gaines later went on to serve in the War of 1812, in which he was awarded a gold medal from Congress.

Photograph reproduced from *The Dictionary of American Portraits*

Brown's Creek Bridge. One of the Army's "improvements" along the Nashville end of the Natchez Trace "government road" still stands today. This bridge, built over Brown's Creek near the ancient Indian village of "Old Town" (see Chapter 2), has weathered many elements, and, except for the span itself, is in excellent condition today.

Photograph courtesy of the United States National Park Service

A National Road

Natchez in the extreme south-western corner of the United States was threatened by Spain in 1800 and later by France and Great Britain.

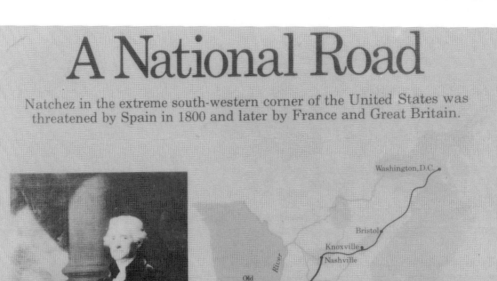

President Jefferson in 1801 decided that a road from Nashville to Natchez was necessary for the safety and welfare of the nation.

Settled Areas 1800
Spanish Lands
Indian Country
— Old Natchez Trace
— Road to Washington, D.C.

"This road being completed, I shall consider our southern extremity secured, the Indians in that quarter at our feet and adjacent province laid open to us."

James Wilkinson

U.S. soldiers built the road.

A National Road. This modern-day exhibit along the Natchez Trace Parkway tells the story of the "national" road days of the Natchez Trace.

View from Fort Adams. In December, 1801, at Fort Adams, the Choctaw Indians gave their approval to the United States Government to construct a post road through their territory in southern Mississippi. A couple of months earlier at the site of today's Memphis, the Chickasaws had given their approval for the road to traverse their lands. These two approvals were sufficient to get the government started on improvement work on the Natchez Trace, which had, by then, been selected to serve as the post road. Fort Adams was perched atop Loftus Heights, and today this dramatic view from the site of the old fort gives a good idea why its strategic location was important to the United States military in the early 1800s.

Photograph courtesy of the United States National Park Service

The Treaty of Fort Adams. This photograph shows a portion of the Treaty of Fort Adams, signed between the chiefs of the Choctaw tribe and commissioners of the United States government. At the meeting which resulted in the treaty, General James Wilkinson, Commander of the Western Department of the United States Army, requested that the federal government be allowed to open a road from Natchez to Nashville. In speaking of the Natchez Trace, the Choctaws agreed that they would "grant a continuance of that road, which may be straightened; but the old path is not to be thrown away entirely, and a new one made." The government's interest, coincidently, was in improving the existing Natchez Trace and not necessarily building a brand new road through the wilderness.

Photograph courtesy of the United States National Park Service

James Wilkinson (1757–1825) was a transplanted Kentuckian who founded Frankfort, the capital of that state. While there, Wilkinson dabbled in land speculation, but by 1787 he had journeyed to New Orleans and had sworn allegiance to the Spanish crown. There he was given the exclusive rights to sell Kentucky produce. Returning to the United States Army in 1789, after an absence of several years, he became the ranking American general by 1797. Wilkinson was involved in the so-called "Spanish conspiracy," a scheme which advocated non-co-operation with the United States confederation by the newly formed western states, thereby leaving them independent to deal with Spain as they wished. It was probably Wilkinson and not Aaron Burr—whom history has branded a traitor—who was really the mastermind behind this Spanish intrigue of the late 1700s and early 1800s. Wilkinson was a key figure in Natchez Trace history for his Spanish con-

nections as well as for his command over the army at the time the improvements were made to the Trace, beginning in 1801.
Photograph courtesy of the United States National Park Service

Garrison Creek. Garrison Creek in Williamson County was so named because of the army troops in garrison there during the days of the Natchez Trace's improvement. From the point where Cunningham's bridge carried the road across Garrison Creek northward into Nashville, the "improved" Trace, sometimes called the "government" road, actually took a different route altogether from the original Indian path. Going south, however, from the point of its crossing of Garrison Creek, the road climbed the ridge and joined the original Trace along the ridgeline, and from there pretty much followed the age-old thoroughfare.
Photograph courtesy of the United States National Park Service

Thomas Hart Benton (1782–1858), who later rose to fame as a U.S. Senator from Missouri, was born in North Carolina and moved to Williamson County, Tennessee, when he was nineteen. With his widowed mother, his brothers and sisters, and the family slaves, he took up residence on a several-thousand-acre estate left by his father. Their house was located on the Natchez Trace "government" road near the Indian boundary line. The community built around the Benton family was appropriately called Bentontown—today's Leiper's Fork.

Drawing from Benton's *Thirty Years' View*

Benton Home. This is the home on the "government" road in which Thomas Hart Benton and his family lived during his Tennessee years, beginning around 1801. The original house no longer stands, and a later home that rested on the old foundations has only recently been destroyed by fire.

Photograph from the Author's collection

Butler's Garrison. Immediately after the treaties were signed with the Chickasaws and the Choctaws, General Wilkinson established two cantonments on the northern end of the Natchez Trace. One was in Williamson County, Tennessee, just on the northern side of the boundary line which separated Indian territory from the State of Tennessee. Colonel Thomas S. Butler was placed in command of this camp. This official National Park Service photograph shows the site identified as *possibly* being that of Colonel Butler's garrison.

Photograph courtesy of the United States National Park Service

Letter to President Jefferson. By 1806, the Natchez Trace had already been used for several years as a post road. In August of that year, the postmaster-general of the United States wrote to President Thomas Jefferson describing the Trace as it was a couple of years after the improvements were completed. A part of the letter is reproduced here. The postmaster-general divided the Trace's length into four parts and outlined the condition of each. He indicated that the seventy miles from Natchez to Grindstone Ford was in "decent order and requires no expenditure." The next forty miles, between Grindstone Ford and Snake Creek "has been cut by the Military and cleared off for a very considerable width, much greater than is necessary for the public service, but some expenditure will be necessary to clear off the under brush and to make the passage of the waters convenient & secure." From Snake Creek to Buffalo Creek, forty miles south of the Tennessee River, the Trace was "entirely in a wilderness state." Finally, the Postmaster reported that from Buffalo Creek to Nash-

ville, a distance of 154 miles, was in need of "an expenditure to remove the undergrowth and to facilitate the passage over the water."

Photograph courtesy of the United States National Park Service

The Postrider. The postrider's job was a tough one indeed. The rider would leave Nashville at eight o'clock on Saturday night, and ten days and four hours later the mail was due in Natchez! The return trip required three weeks. The mail consisted of a few letters, some government dispatches, and several newspapers. For his own use, the rider carried a blanket, a half bushel of corn, and a tin trumpet to sound his arrival. An account taken from the recollections of one of the first postriders to use the Natchez Trace indicates that he would "leave Nashville and pass Tom Davis' (the last white man's house, which stood near where Franklin now is) at midnight. Sunday morning he would set to Gordon's Ferry, on Duck River, fifty-one miles from Nashville. . . . He then had a ride eighty miles to Colbert's Ferry, on the Tennessee river; before night set in, where the Indians would set him across. . . . Then. . . he would have to go to the Chickasaw Agency, one hundred and twenty miles before he

would see a house. . . . From the Chickasaw to the Choctaw Agency the distance was two hundred miles . . . through Indian country . . . from this point to Natchez was one hundred miles."

Drawing reproduced from an old woodcut

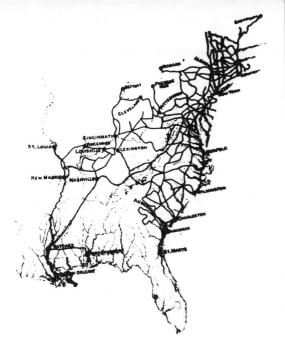

Marble—A quarry of marble has lately been discovered and opened near New Haven, Connecticut—Another quarry of marble has lately been opened in the vicinity of York, Pennsylvania, specimens of which have been sent to Philadelphia for inspection, and declared to be equal to the Italian.

Road from Natchez to Pittsburgh.

To Washington	7	Carpenter's station	10
Selserstown	5	Danville	11
Union Town	8	Kentucky river	12
Huntstown	8	Nicholasville	8
Gibson's port, Biopier	25	Lexington, Kentucky	12
Grindstone ford, Biopier	8	Paris	19
M'Ravens, Indian line	18	Millersburgh	8
Brashear's	40	Blue Lick	13
Norton's	12	May's Lick.	12
Chotas	30	Washington	8
Leffoes	34	Maysville	4
Falsom's, Pigeon Roost	30	January's, Ohio	15
Choctaw Lane	43	Horns	17
Indian Agents	10	Falls of Paint	20
James Colbert's	10	Reaves Crossing	3
Old Factor's	26	Chilicothe	12
James Brown's	17	M'Coys	9
Bear creek	33	Craig's	6
Levi Colberts, Buzzard Roost	5	Pursley's	11
		New Lancaster	11
Geo. Colberts, Ten river	7	Canaway's	8
Toscomby's	16	Beard's	10
Factor's sons	16	Zanesville	12
Indian Lane	20	Brown's	9
Dobbin's	5	Morrison's	5
Stanfield's, Keg Spring	8	Spear's	4
Duck river	8	Will's creek	8
Smith's	8	Henry Beamer's	6
Boon's	16	Smith's	5
Franklin	8	Wherry's Branch, Ca.	5
M'Donalds	6	Enslow's	8
Nashville, Tennessee	12	M'Donald's	9
State line	35	St. Clairsville	7
Barren court-house	35	Wheeling	10
Burks	11	Reefer's	6
Little Barren river	2	Alexandria	10
Greensburgh	12	M'Cracken's	7
Abraham Hardens	13	Washington	10
Munn's powder mill	8	Canonsburgh	7
Nash's mill	11	Pittsburgh	18
		Total to Pittsburgh—1,013	

Main Post Roads. As this map indicates, the Natchez Trace was the only post road in the entire south-central portion of the United States in 1804. While traffic and trade in the industrialized northeast and along the heavily settled eastern shore had many alternative routes to follow, the Tennessee–Mississippi country had little other choice but to use the old Indian trail—improved over the years—which linked Nashville to Natchez.

Drawing reproduced from the *Natchez Trace Parkway Survey*

Natchez Trace Inns. A page from an old almanac lists the stands, or inns, which operated between Natchez and Nashville during the early 1800s. Even though the stands sprang up randomly along the Trace's length—most likely when a settler along the route wanted to add to his meager income by providing food and lodging for passing travelers—it turned out that they were nicely spaced about a day or so's journey apart.

Photograph courtesy of the United States National Park Service

Accommodations along the Trace. Although primitive by today's standards, the stands did offer hot food and protection at night from the elements. When the food was ready for the evening's meal, it was placed on a big table and all of the guests helped themselves "family-style." Some travelers, however, still preferred the elements to the stands. In 1816, a minister who traveled the Trace complained that some of the "hotels are made of small poles, just high enough for you to stand straight in, with a dirt floor, no bedding of any kind, except a bearskin, and not that in some of these huts. You feel blank and disappointed when you walk in and find a cold dirt floor, naked walls and no fire. Camping out is far better than such accommodations."

Drawing reproduced from an old woodcut

McIntoshville, or Tokshish, was the home of John McIntosh, the Indian agent for the British government, and is among the oldest sites on the Natchez Trace. Francis Baily stopped by McIntosh's on his way up the Trace in 1797. In time, a settlement grew around McIntosh's farm, and by 1805 a traveler wrote that there were "six well-improved farms, made by White men & natives who are in the habit of farming after the mode of the whites; & vend their supplies to travelers." In later years, Tokshish became the site of a missionary school. By the time the Natchez Trace Parkway survey was made in the 1930s and 1940s, this slave cabin was one of the few remaining buildings in the complex.

Photograph courtesy of the United States National Park Service

Buzzard's Roost. One of the most famous stands along the Natchez Trace was known as Buzzard's Roost and was owned by Levi Colbert, a Chickasaw chief, who had the insight to capitalize on the increasing traffic up and down the Trace. An astute businessman, Levi, in addition to running his hostelry, owned substantial property in the area, including farms, salt springs, grist mills, and slaves.

Photograph courtesy of the United States National Park Service

Gordon's Ferry. Another sizeable river for the traveler to contend with was the Duck, over which the Tennessee end of the Natchez Trace crossed. Although not as wide as the Tennessee River, the Duck was large enough, especially during the rainy season, to require a ferry. John Gordon established Gordon's Ferry there and operated it until his death in 1819. Records exist today which indicate that John Gordon charged $112.50 in May, 1815, for ferrying 1,800 soldiers of the Kentucky Militia across the Duck River. The site of Gordon's Ferry has this appearance today.
Photograph courtesy of the United States National Park Service

The Gordon House. John Gordon built a substantial house on his property along the Duck River. His land holdings there had been obtained by land grant for "meritorious deeds in many hazardous undertakings among the Indians." This view shows the Gordon House as it appeared in recent years, with the Natchez Trace passing in front of the house, after having crossed the Duck River at Gordon's Ferry to the left. Nashville is to the right.
Photograph courtesy of the United States National Park Service

Colbert's Ferry. During the heyday of the Natchez Trace, George Colbert's ferry provided the only practical way to cross the Tennessee River. Colbert was described by a contemporary as the most influential chief in the Chickasaw nation. "He is an artful designing man more for his own interest, than that of his nation. . . ," he wrote. Another observer reported that Colbert "very much influences the affairs of that (Chickasaw) nation." Like his brother, Levi, George was a shrewd businessman, and the story goes that he charged a handsome $75,000 for transporting Andrew Jackson's troops across the Tennessee river in 1815!
Photograph courtesy of the United States National Park Service

Gordon Monument. John Gordon, the owner of Gordon's Ferry and the Gordon House, was an old Indian fighter and had a distinguished record for conspicuous service during the Coldwater and Nickajack expeditions in 1787 and 1794 against the renegade Cherokees who lived along the Tennessee River. Gordon was also the first postmaster of Nashville, and today this monument on the grounds of Nashville's old Post Office honors the man and his contributions to the survival of the Middle Tennessee settlement during its infancy.

Photograph by James A. Crutchfield

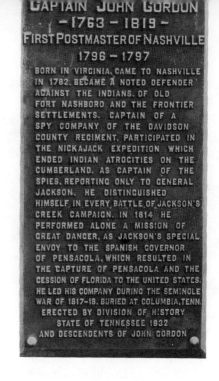

CAPTAIN JOHN GORDON
-1763 - 1819 -
FIRST POSTMASTER OF NASHVILLE
1796 - 1797
BORN IN VIRGINIA, CAME TO NASHVILLE IN 1782. BECAME A NOTED DEFENDER AGAINST THE INDIANS, OF OLD FORT NASHBORO AND THE FRONTIER SETTLEMENTS. CAPTAIN OF A SPY COMPANY OF THE DAVIDSON COUNTY REGIMENT, PARTICIPATED IN THE NICKAJACK EXPEDITION WHICH ENDED INDIAN ATROCITIES ON THE CUMBERLAND. AS CAPTAIN OF THE SPIES, REPORTING ONLY TO GENERAL JACKSON, HE DISTINGUISHED HIMSELF IN EVERY BATTLE OF JACKSON'S CREEK CAMPAIGN. IN 1814 HE PERFORMED ALONE A MISSION OF GREAT DANGER, AS JACKSON'S SPECIAL ENVOY TO THE SPANISH GOVERNOR OF PENSACOLA, WHICH RESULTED IN THE CAPTURE OF PENSACOLA AND THE CESSION OF FLORIDA TO THE UNITED STATES. HE LED HIS COMPANY DURING THE SEMINOLE WAR OF 1817-18. BURIED AT COLUMBIA, TENN. ERECTED BY DIVISION OF HISTORY STATE OF TENNESSEE 1932 AND DESCENDENTS OF JOHN GORDON

Washington Hotel. In time, a little more sophistication—comparable to that of hotels elsewhere in the old Southwest—appeared among some of the inns along the Natchez Trace. But this occurred primarily in the villages and towns which sat astride the Trace, and not among those stands in the wilderness. The attractive and spacious Washington Hotel operated between 1808 and 1817 in Washington, Mississippi.

Photograph from *Mount Locust on the Old Natchez Trace*

Colbert's Stand. Not far from Levi Colbert's inn stood another stand, this one owned by Levi's brother, George. George Colbert also operated the ferry across the Tennessee River. Colbert's Stand in later years was photographed, and a reproduction of the original picture is shown here. In time, the old house was destroyed by fire, and for years only the stone chimney stood, lonely and vigilant, overlooking the old Trace which passed nearby.

Photograph courtesy of the United States National Park Service

Aaron Burr (1756–1836), the vice-president of the United States under Thomas Jefferson, was a frequent visitor to Nashville and the environs of the Natchez Trace. A very popular figure until a smear campaign by Jefferson cast doubts about his patriotism, Burr quickly fell from the popular eye. In 1807, Burr was traveling as a private citizen in the Mississippi Territory, a wanted man by the United States government. The charge was treason, Burr having been accused of conspiring with Spain to annex the western part of the United States. Recent evidence has suggested that Burr might have been framed on this charge, and that the real culprit was another figure frequently associated with Natchez Trace history, General James Wilkinson. Wilkinson, the commanding general of the United States Army at the time, actually served as a secret agent for the Spanish government for twenty years.

Portrait from Parton's *Life of Aaron Burr*

Nicholas Perkins. On February 18, 1807, Nicholas Perkins was the registrar of the Wakefield, Mississippi, land office. During the evening of that day, a man Perkins identified as Aaron Burr rode by his door. The next day Perkins, assisted by Lieutenant Edmund Pendleton Gaines and a few United States soldiers, arrested Burr and eventually accompanied him to Richmond, Virginia, where he stood trial and was acquitted. This occasion marked the second time that Burr had been in trouble with the law in the area. He had been apprehended the first time the month before and had been carried to Washington, Mississippi, to be heard by a grand jury. Burr was not indicted then, but the wily politician had left town before he could be formally dismissed. Perkins actually caught Burr while he was a fugitive from justice after his quick departure from Washington.

Photograph courtesy of Caro [Mrs. Sam] Woolwine, Martha [Mrs. Perkins] Trousdale, and Leighla [Mrs. Lester, Jr.] Carroll

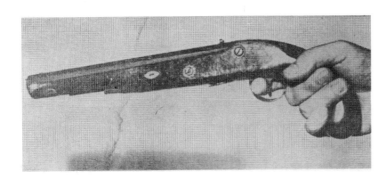

Burr Pistol. This pistol, once belonging to Aaron Burr, was confiscated from him by Nicholas Perkins when he arrested the ex-vice-president in 1807.

Photograph courtesy of Mrs. Woolwine, Mrs. Trousdale, and Mrs. Carroll

Harmon Blennerhasset (1765–1831), one of Aaron Burr's strangest disciples, lived on his own private island in the middle of the Ohio River. Blennerhasset joined Burr in the so-called "Spanish conspiracy" and assisted the ex-vice-president with moral encouragement as well as with money. Concerning his journey up the Natchez Trace on his way to Burr's trial in Richmond, he wrote of "myriads of mosquitoes and horseflies," and he described Nashville as "very dull and ugly but tolerably cheap." Blennerhasset bought—and lived in for several years—a plantation near the Natchez Trace at Port Gibson. He later moved to Canada and then to the Isle of Guernsey, where he died.

Portrait from Roosevelt's *Winning of the West*

Lorenzo Dow (1777–1834) was one of the more famous preachers to travel the Natchez Trace. Dow, a Methodist minister from Connecticut, was known throughout the region as the "crazy preacher" because of his rather eccentric and bizarre mannerisms. "Pale, sallow, and somewhat consumptive in the appearance of his countenance; dressed in the plainest attire, with his single-breasted coat, often worn threadbare . . . his whole appearance was one such as to awaken a high degree of curiosity and interest." Dow journeyed up and down the Trace several times, and he kept a journal of his wanderings that has become a valuable source of information about the region and its times.

Photograph courtesy of the United States National Park Service

Montpier. Nicholas Perkins received a reward of $3,331 for his arrest of Aaron Burr, and, sometime after this incident, he migrated to Williamson County, Tennessee. There he built this magnificent home, *Montpier*, overlooking the "government road" section of the improved Natchez Trace in Williamson County.

Photograph courtesy of the United States National Park Service

Camp Meeting. The old Southwest was a hotbed of religious activity in the early 1800s, and no doubt the convenience of the Natchez Trace and its use by the preachers and the missionaries did much to spread the gospel. Camp meetings, such as the one pictured, became prevalent throughout much of Tennessee, Kentucky, and Mississippi during the years of the Natchez Trace's popularity. People came from miles around to attend one of these religious exercises at a time when there were not enough preachers for regularly scheduled services. A contemporary observer of one of these meetings described participants as "jerking all over . . . and the more they resisted, the more they jerked."

Drawing from Goodrich's *Recollections of a Lifetime*

Itinerant Preacher. During the middle and later years of the Natchez Trace's popularity, itinerant preachers and missionaries to the Indians were among the most frequent users of the thoroughfare. The Chickasaws and Choctaws were prime targets for the zealous churchmen of the old Southwest, and the Natchez Trace provided the most direct way to travel to the Indians' homeland.

Engraving reproduced from *The American Revolution—A Picture Sourcebook*

The Aaron Burr oaks, on the grounds of Jefferson College in Washington, Mississippi, derived their name from the fact that Burr was presented to a grand jury nearby in 1807. Burr was not indicted and he quickly left the scene, only to be apprehended again and taken to Richmond for trial.

Photograph courtesy of the United States National Park Service

Meriwether Lewis. One of the most tragic events to occur along the Natchez Trace during its "national" era was the death of Meriwether Lewis. Lewis, of the famed Lewis and Clark expedition to the Pacific Ocean, was en route to Washington on the Natchez Trace when he rode up to Grinder's Stand in October, 1809, to spend the evening. Sometime during the night Lewis screamed out, and Mrs. Grinder, the wife of the inn-owner, entered his room to find him in agony, shot in the head. Lewis died shortly afterwards. The debate still goes on as to whether his death was murder or suicide. This painting shows Lewis as he approached Grinder's stand from the south.

Painting courtesy of the United States Highway Commission

Meriwether Lewis (1774–1809), before his brief life was snuffed out at Grinder's Stand, had been the leader of the Lewis and Clark Expedition, and earlier had served as Thomas Jefferson's personal secretary. After the return of his expedition to the Pacific Ocean, Lewis was appointed Governor of Louisiana, the vast territory purchased from France in 1803. In 1809, Lewis had left his headquarters in St. Louis to travel to Washington. His plans were to go down the Mississippi River to New Orleans, and to travel to the capital by ship around Florida. Somewhere on the Mississippi River near Chickasaw Bluffs (today's Memphis), he decided to leave the river and cut overland to the Natchez Trace and to follow it to Nashville, thence overland to Washington.

Portrait from *Pageant of America*

Log Building near Grinder's Stand. Today this modern log building stands near the site of Grinder's Stand where Meriwether Lewis died.

Photograph courtesy of the United States National Park Service

Criminals along the Trace. Highwaymen and outlaws had been common enough along the Natchez Trace during the "boatmen's" era, but with the advent of the "national road," brigands seemed to multiply. Even though soldiers were placed along the route from time to time, ostensibly for the protection of travelers, it is doubtful that they accomplished much in the way of reducing the rate of robberies, murders, and other heinous crimes.

Picture reproduced from Phares' *Reverend Devil*

Alexander Wilson (1766–1813), the renowned ornithologist and artist and a friend of Meriwether Lewis, made a trip through Nashville and then down the Natchez Trace in 1810, just months after the bizarre death of his friend. While Wilson's primary mission was to identify and paint new species of birds, he took it upon himself to personally investigate the circumstances of Lewis's death. The Grinders still owned the inn, and Wilson interviewed Mrs. Grinder at length. After leaving some money for the erection of a fence around Lewis's nearby grave, Wilson departed the vicinity convinced that his friend had been murdered.

Portrait from the painting by Rembrandt Peale

Meriwether Lewis Monument. In 1848, the State of Tennessee erected a monument to Meriwether Lewis at the place of his death. Symbolic of Lewis's brief life, the gravestone displays a broken shaft. In 1843, Tennessee also honored Lewis when it established a new county, encompassing the area where he died, and named it Lewis County.

Photograph by Regena H. Crutchfield

Murrell Disposing of a Body.
This old picture shows John Murrell and an associate disposing of the body of one of their victims along the Natchez Trace.

Picture from Coates' *The Outlaw Years*

John A. Murrell. One of the most notorious outlaws of the Natchez Trace was John A. Murrell, a native of Williamson County, Tennessee. Although he worked the Trace after the "national" period, he was representative of the outlaws who flourished during the heyday of the Trace. According to Murrell's own words, his father "was an honest man I expect, and tried to raise me honest; but I think none the better of him for that. My mother was of the pure grit: she learnt me and all her children to steal so soon as we could walk, and would hide for us whenever she could." Murrell's specialty was slave snatching, in which he stole a slave, usually with his co-operation on the premise of conducting him to a free state. Before the slave realized it, however, he had been sold and re-stolen several times, never obtaining his promised freedom. On one occasion, "The old Negro man became suspicious that we were going to sell them, and became quite contrary. . . . I shot him through the head, and then ripped open his belly and tumbled him into the river!" Active in the wilderness between Nashville and Natchez, Murrell was finally caught, tried, and sentenced to the Tennessee State Prison in Nashville.

Picture from "The Life and Times of John A. Murrell," *Police Gazette*

Branding a Criminal. Punishment on the frontier could be harsh, and on the few occasions when highwaymen and outlaws were brought to justice, they paid dearly for their crimes. This woodcut shows a criminal being branded with the letters, "HT," for horse thief, on his left thumb. In addition to this punishment, he received twenty lashes, six months' imprisonment, and was required to stand before public ridicule in the pillory for two hours on each of three days. The charge? Stealing a horse valued at $120!

Picture reproduced from an old woodcut

Jackson's Troops Returning to Nashville. One of the most important roles which the Natchez Trace played was its service to the military establishment. As early as 1803–1804, volunteer troops from Tennessee had marched down the Trace in anticipation of possible trouble during the transfer of the Louisiana Purchase to American ownership. Later, during the War of 1812, Andrew Jackson offered the services of 2,500 Tennessee militiamen to the federal forces, and the cavalry followed the Natchez Trace to Washington, Mississippi, while the infantry, under Jackson himself, took the river route. After the army had departed Nashville, General Wilkinson wrote to Jackson from Mississippi telling him not to bring the troops down, and on March 15, 1813, Jackson received official communications from the War Department ordering him to disband his army. The angered Jackson financed, with his own funds, the trip back to Nashville over the Trace. In fact, it was his determined will to personally supervise the safe return of his troops—many by now sick and dying from the severe elements—that earned him the name, "Old Hickory" by his admiring followers, who said he was "as tough as hickory." The last important use of the Natchez Trace as a military road was when Jackson's troops returned from the Battle of New Orleans in 1815.

Drawing by Charles Young, courtesy of *Cumberland Magazine*

The Original Log Hermitage. Andrew Jackson returned to this home and his beloved Rachel in Nashville after his service in the War of 1812. The original "Hermitage" was a simple log home. Several years later Jackson built the magnificent mansion of the same name nearby. The log "Hermitage" is a monument to the pre-presidential period of Jackson's life.

Drawing by James A. Crutchfield

Thomas Jefferson. Although Jefferson College was the namesake of Thomas Jefferson (1743–1826), the president never saw the school, and he never traveled the Natchez Trace. Yet he had a profound influence on the thoroughfare and its times. Jefferson figured prominently in the chapters of Trace history which pertained to its improvement by the United States Army, the Aaron Burr episode, and the Meriwether Lewis tragedy.

Painting by Charles W. Peale

Jefferson College. Jefferson College, located on the lower Natchez Trace in Washington, Mississippi, was incorporated in 1802 by the first General Assembly of the Mississippi Territory, but it did not open for business until 1811, and even then it offered only preparatory school courses. By 1817, however, it had become a college as originally planned, and it operated continuously until 1863, when the War Between the States forced its closing. Re-opening in 1866, again as a preparatory school, it maintained its charter until its final closing in 1964. Names for President Thomas Jefferson, the college numbered many notables as its students, including the future president of the Confederate States of America, Jefferson Davis. Today, Historic Jefferson College is listed on the National Register and is maintained by the Mississippi Department of Archives and History.

Photograph by Regena H. Crutchfield

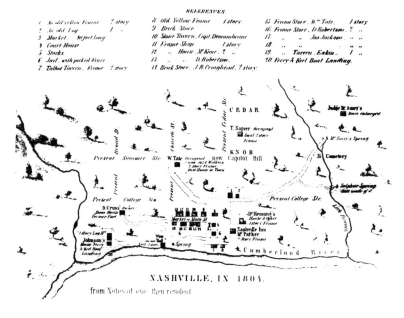

Early Nashville. During the time of the government improvement of the Natchez Trace, Nashville was still a small village, and, as late as the first decade of the 1800s, contained only a few houses. This map, of the town during those early days, graphically depicts its rural nature some twenty-four years after its settlement. Nashville soon became the most important English-speaking town in the Tennessee–Kentucky territory. There were apparently good accommodations to be had in Nashville, the writings of some travelers notwithstanding. In 1797, Francis Baily, the Englishman who journeyed up the Natchez Trace from Natchez, mentioned several taverns, and records indicate that the Nashville Inn, the City Hotel, and Talbot's Hotel were all early hostelries located on the public square.

Map reproduced from Putnam's *History of Middle Tennessee*

Elizabeth Female Academy. One of the last institutions to be associated with the Natchez Trace, prior to its loss of prominence as the leading highway in the old Southwest, was the Elizabeth Female Academy. Organized in 1818, in Washington, Mississippi, the school is believed to have been the first chartered institution for the higher education of females in the South. Study courses included natural philosophy, chemistry, Latin, botany, and classical subjects. John James Audubon, the eminent American ornithologist and painter, was among the faculty members at the academy. In 1845, the Elizabeth Female Academy closed its doors forever, a victim of the state's shift of population from the Natchez region to the northeast around the capital of Jackson. Only

one brick wall remains today of this once outstanding school for young females.
Photograph courtesy of the United States National Park Service

Natchez Riverfront. Natchez, on the other end of the Natchez Trace, fared as well as, or better than, Nashville. Its strategic location on the Mississippi River made it a natural market for the increasing cotton production in the southern portion of Mississippi. After the advent of the steamboat, the town became even more important as a stop on the way down the Mississippi River to New Orleans. While the Natchez Trace was doomed for obsolescence, its two most important towns—Natchez and Nashville—had firmly established themselves as key cities in the old Southwest.
Picture from *Pageant of America*

Tennessee's first state capitol building. By 1815, Nashville had the population and the influence to have the state capital moved there for a few years before it was permanently located in the city in 1843. This building, situated on the corner of today's Eighth Avenue and Broadway, served as the first capitol building for Tennessee government in Nashville. By the time of the Natchez Trace's decline as a popular thoroughfare, the towns at both ends and along its way had established their own importance in the region.
Drawing by James A. Crutchfield

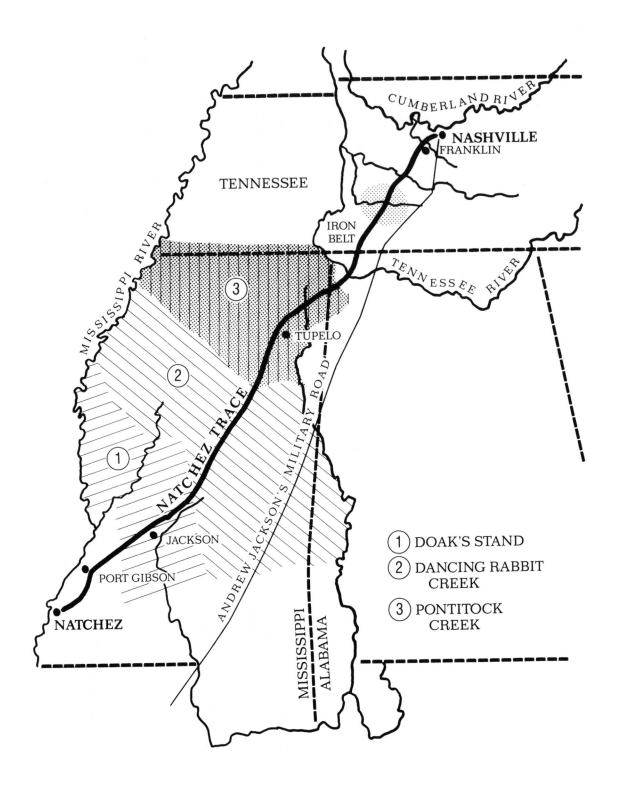

CUMBERLAND RIVER

NASHVILLE
FRANKLIN

TENNESSEE

MISSISSIPPI RIVER

IRON
BELT

TENNESSEE RIVER

③

TUPELO

②

NATCHEZ TRACE

①

ANDREW JACKSON'S MILITARY ROAD

JACKSON

PORT GIBSON

NATCHEZ

MISSISSIPPI
ALABAMA

① DOAK'S STAND
② DANCING RABBIT
    CREEK
③ PONTITOCK
    CREEK

CHAPTER EIGHT
Years of Neglect

Highways, like the vehicles which travel upon them, have their own life cycles and are quickly forgotten when newer, more modern replacements come along. The interstate highway system, christened in the Eisenhower administration as being the ultimate in road design, is already outdated. The dramatic increase in personal travel and commercial transportation in America has made it difficult to devise a highway system to handle the faster and more voluminous traffic.

It was no different with the Natchez Trace. As soon as it was discovered that there was a faster way to make the trip from Natchez to Nashville, the old Trace became obsolete. That faster way, which was causing eyebrows to raise and tongues to wag, was the steamboat. During the previous years, while floating goods *downstream* on American inland waterways was a simple enough solution to getting goods to market, the impracticality, difficulty, and slowness of rowing or poling a flatboat back *upstream* in order to get home, were overwhelming. But with the steamboat paddling its way upstream at a whopping three miles per hour, the days of subjecting oneself to the heat,

Natchez Trace—1820–1840. After the demise of the Natchez Trace as a major thoroughfare, the old path fell into disrepair. Jackson's military road did much to shorten the time of travel between Nashville and New Orleans, and since speed was of the essence in moving military troops back and forth across the new frontier, it was only natural that the Natchez Trace's popularity waned in favor of the shorter, faster, more modern military road. Three Indian treaties—at Doak's Stand on October 18, 1820; at Dancing Rabbit Creek on September 27 and 28, 1830; and at Pontitock Creek on October 20, 1832—took the remaining lands of the Choctaws and Chickasaws and sent the two tribes to the region beyond the Mississippi River. The War Between the States played no large role in the development or the decline of the Natchez Trace, but several battles were fought along its length. Iron had been discovered in the early 1800s along the Middle Tennessee portion of the Trace, and for many years the red ore provided a valuable source of income to several smelters in this part of the region.

Drawing by James A. Crutchfield and Edison Travelstead

cold, insects, snakes, outlaws, and other horrors of the wilderness were over.

In 1811, Nicholas Roosevelt, a progenitor of the famous New York Roosevelt clan, plied down the Ohio and Mississippi Rivers from Pittsburgh to New Orleans aboard his steamboat, the *New Orleans*. Built at a cost of $40,000, the *New Orleans* soon started earning its keep by carrying goods between New Orleans and Natchez. Amidst the "oohs" and "ahs" of the spectators along its route as the *New Orleans* steamed into port, the boat must have seemed like the final answer to their transportation woes. But old habits die hard, and as one social historian has said, ". . . so abrupt and uncanny was the contrast between the steamboat and the craft she was intended to supplant that the public held aloof from her in the bestowal of their patronage until several trips had been made. She seemed too much of a miracle, at first, and many travellers and merchants preferred to use the barges and flatboats with which they were familiar until the new system of transportation had somewhat demonstrated its reliability in practise." Success was not long in coming, however, and the flatboats and keelboats were dropped rapidly in favor of the much faster and more efficient steamboat.

As if to add insult to injury, the year 1820 saw the completion of a new road system designed to shorten the trip between Nashville and New Orleans. The Natchez Trace and its extension south of Natchez spanned 736 miles between the two towns, and Andrew Jackson's Millitary Road, as the new highway was called, cut about 220 miles from this distance. The new road was a definite asset in fostering better communications with the southwestern part of the country. As a result of the completion of the military road with its 35-foot-wide roadbed, along with the already proven success of the steamboat in moving people and goods both downstream and upstream in a minimum of time, the Natchez Trace took its last breath as a viable communications link for the rapidly growing United States.

With the Natchez Trace no longer an important artery of commerce and communication between Nashville and parts to the southwest, the region which bordered the old thoroughfare lapsed into an anonymity that was to last for more than 100 years. Through disuse, the Trace reverted to wilderness along much of its way. Had it not been for the deep, well-worn tracks made by centuries of constant use by the buffalo, the Indians, and the whites, the forest might have reclaimed all vestiges of this once popular and much traveled road. When it could be justified by local authorities, sections of its length here and there were maintained and utilized as county roads. Otherwise, the famous Natchez Trace became just another memory in the minds of the few people who could still remember what it was like to travel over its dark, dangerous course.

The War Between the States came and passed and in so doing left its mark upon the people and places associated with the Natchez Trace. Several skirmishes and battles took place at Natchez, Port Gibson, Tupelo, Franklin, and Nashville. But the Trace itself played no important role in the great conflict. Reconstruction and its attendant miseries brought a new era of pain and suffering to the residents of the region, but when it was all over the old road had simply taken the War and its aftermath in stride.

During the 1800s and on into the first quarter of the present century, iron mining and smelting constituted a profitable business along the Tennessee end of the Natchez Trace. As early as the 1820s, a good grade of iron ore had been discovered in that region, and for around 100 years the industry provided livelihoods for many local residents. With the discovery of richer ore fields elsewhere, coupled with the advent of more modern and economical technologies with which to extract the iron, this industry—like the Natchez Trace itself—passed into oblivion.

In the early 1900s, several articles about the Trace were printed in popular journals. One in particular, written by John Swain and appearing in *Everybody's Magazine* in 1905, is credited with providing inspiration for successfully popularizing the Natchez Trace. Thanks to these articles, along with the Daughters of the American Revolution and the Daughters of the War of 1812, a campaign was begun—although not thought of as a movement at the time—to make people more aware of the existence of the old Natchez Trace and the role it played in the history of the original Southwest. The Daughters of the American Revolution erected monuments in practically every county through which the Trace ran in Mississippi, Alabama, and Tennessee, while the Daughters of the War of 1812 erected its own tributes in Tennessee.

By the time of Franklin Delano Roosevelt's New Deal and its search for public projects which would serve the dual purposes of putting Americans back to work during and after the Depression, while at the same time providing something meaningful for posterity, the Natchez Trace and its place in history were once again in the consciousness of many southerners. It was up to one of them, United States Representative Jeff Busby of Mississippi, to set the wheels in motion for the creation and implementation of a fitting memorial to the Natchez Trace and one which has subsequently become a most important link in today's National Park system.

The *New Orleans*, Roosevelt's steamboat, was the first steam-powered vessel to travel the Ohio and Mississippi Rivers. From the time of that famous journey onward, the course of history was changed. No longer were the rivers' fickle currents a problem in negotiating their courses, either upstream or down. No longer were hours of arm and back breaking poling and paddling required to move a vessel a few miles upriver. But the new contraptions had their disadvantages, too. The pressures which built up in the boilers were extremely dangerous if overdone, and there was always the chance that the superstructure would catch fire from the sparks coming out of the smokestacks. Finally, the river itself—with low and high waters, tree snags, and floating debris—made travel especially risky in these pressurized, explosion-prone hulks.

Picture from *Pageant of America*

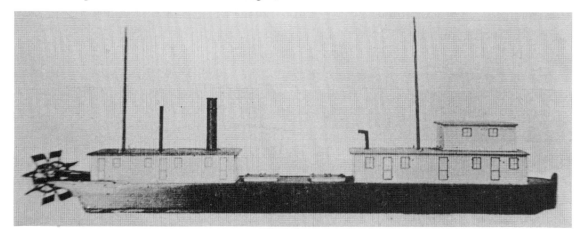

Nicholas Roosevelt (1767–1854) was employed in 1809 by the steamboat pioneer Robert Fulton to reconnoiter the Ohio and Mississippi Rivers to determine if steamboats could be utilized for trade and transportation on the two streams. Roosevelt combined his business with his honeymoon, and he and Mrs. Roosevelt returned to Pittsburgh in 1810 after having traveled downstream to New Orleans for six months aboard a flatboat. His response to Fulton was positive, and on October 1, 1811, he sailed again from Pittsburgh aboard the newly built steamboat the *New Orleans*. After being caught in the middle of the New Madrid earthquake which created Reelfoot Lake, he finally reached Natchez. By January, 1812, the *New Orleans* was making regular trips between New Orleans and Natchez and charging twenty-five dollars for the upriver journey and eighteen dollars for the trip downstream. After proving that steamboat traffic was a natural for American inland waterways, thereby directly causing the obsolescence of the Natchez Trace, the *New Orleans* sank two years later after running into a stump near Baton Rouge.

Portrait from the Nicholas G. Roosevelt Collection, reproduced from *The Dictionary of American Portraits*

Jackson's Military Road. After the War of 1812 was won, the United States Government determined that its road system needed vast improvements to meet the communications and transportation requirements of the rapidly growing country. In 1817, the first major project, "General Jackson's Military Road," was undertaken. Between Columbia, Tennessee, and Madisonville, Louisiana—located across Lake Pontchartrain from New Orleans—the right of way was cleared to a width of 40 feet to make room for the 35-foot roadbed. Over 300 men were employed in the road's construction, and before the task was completed, 35 bridges had been built, along with 20,000 feet of causeway. The total tab for the project amounted to around $300,000. The United States Army was employed to assist in the job, and over 75,000 man-days of labor over a three year period were expended. As archaic as these improvements seem to us today, in its own time—when compared to the old Natchez Trace—the Jackson military road must have seemed like a superhighway.

Picture courtesy of the Federal Highway Administration

Pushmataha (1764–1824) was the Choctaw chief who represented his tribe at the Doak's Stand Treaty in October, 1820. For several weeks the Choctaw and American delegations met and bargained over the five million acres of Mississippi land which the Choctaws had and the Americans wanted. Andrew Jackson, representing the United States Government, promised 13 million acres of land across the Mississippi River in exchange for the Choctaws' property, which, in fact, was only a portion of what the tribe claimed in the state. Finally, after several days of arguing back and forth, Jackson's famous temper got the best of him and he threatened either extinction of the Choctaws or their forcible movement to the new western lands. The Choctaws gave in, and the first chapter of the shameful Indian removal tragedy was begun. One of the most lasting effects the Treaty had on the white population of Mississippi was the removal of the capital from Natchez to LeFleur's Bluff, renamed Jackson, in 1822.

Picture from McKenney and Hall, *Indian Tribes of North America*

Site of the Treaty of Dancing Rabbit Creek. Not satisfied with the shady dealings perpetrated on the Choctaws at Doak's Stand in 1820, the Mississippi legislature in 1830 denied all native rights of Indians living within the state, and in their place, extended the state's rights. In so doing, the way was paved for the final removal of the red man from Mississippi soil. In late September, 1830, the Americans, represented by John Eaton and John Coffee, two of Andrew Jackson's protégés, met with the Choctaws at Dancing Rabbit Creek. There, with the whisk of a pen, the Indians signed away the remainder of their southeastern homeland.

Photograph courtesy of the United States National Park Service

John Catron (1786–1865) was one of the first men to recognize the importance of the iron ore banks along the Natchez Trace in Tennessee. During the 1820s and 1830s, Catron was one of the principal promoters of activities in the area. Born in Pennsylvania, Catron served with Andrew Jackson in the War of 1812 and later practiced law in Nashville. He was a judge on the Tennessee Supreme Court of Errors and Appeals from 1824 until 1836, and in 1837, President Martin Van Buren appointed him an Associate Justice of the United States Supreme Court, a post he held until his death. Catron preceded the people who gave their name to the mining activities of the region, the Napiers, by several years.

Engraving by Frederick Girsch, reproduced from *The Dictionary of American Portraits*

Napier Mine. One of the largest iron mines in the vicinity—and one which sat directly beside the Natchez Trace—was the Napier Mine, located just south of the Metal Ford on the Buffalo River. The original deed to the ore bank was granted in 1826, and the open pit mine was worked for nearly 100 years before it closed operations in the 1920s. The procedures for extracting the ore at this mine were relatively simple. It was first removed from the surface of the ground as it was exposed, and mule-drawn wagons then took the ore out of the pit to an area where men using 25-pound hammers reduced the large pieces to a size manageable by the smelting operations. The ore at Napier was extremely rich, containing in some cases over fifty per cent iron.

Photgraph courtesy of the United States National Park Service

Cedar Grove Furnace. Furnaces such as this one were utilized along the Natchez Trace during the heyday of iron ore production there. These furnaces, known as cold-blast furnaces, used water from the nearby Buffalo River to drive the bellows which in turn allowed for the production of a better draft than was possible with hand bellows. Over fifteen tons of iron a week could be produced with this type furnace. The photograph shows the Cedar Grove Furnace in nearby Perry County, Tennessee.

Photograph courtesy of the United States National Park Service

The Metal Ford Mill Race was on the Buffalo River adjacent to the Natchez Trace. The mill race was used as a channel to divert water out of the river to the nearby blast furnaces. There the water was used to power the bellows which created the draft required to maintain the intense temperatures necessary in the smelting of the iron ore.

Photograph courtesy of the United States National Park Service

Natchez "On the Hill." By 1830, the State of Mississippi had over 136,000 inhabitants, nearly half of whom were slaves. Only around 3000 people lived in an urban environment at the time, and among the few villages of any size was Natchez. Once the capital of both the Mississippi Territory and the state, Natchez lost its preeminence when the seat of government was moved in the 1820s to Jackson. This scene depicts Natchez "on the hill"— as opposed to the infamous Natchez "under the hill"—as it appeared looking from the site of Fort Rosalie in the 1830s.

Picture from a lithograph by Pifeo H. Browne

Bayou Pierre Bridge. In the old days of the Natchez Trace, Bayou Pierre was the last point reached going north from Natchez before the unknown of the wilderness was confronted. In May, 1863, the retreating Confederate Army burned the bridge spanning the bayou at Grindstone Ford, thus forcing its Union pursuers to seek alternative means of crossing. This old photograph shows the rebuilt bridge over the bayou as it appeared when the Natchez Trace Parkway survey was made during the 1930s and 1940s.

Photograph courtesy of the United States National Park Service

Nashville occupied by the Federal Army in February, 1862. Already a sizable town, its location provided the Federals a springboard from which they could leap across the entire Middle Tennessee region. This scene shows the town looking north toward the State Capitol in the middle background. Almost three years after occupation, the last major battle of the War Between the States was fought at Nashville, resulting in the disastrous rout of General John Bell Hood's Army of Tennessee and a signal victory for Union General George Thomas.

Picture from *Harper's Pictorial History of the Civil War*

Windsor Plantation. While not a casualty of the War Between the States, the ruins of *Windsor* near Port Gibson, Mississippi, give one the eerie feeling that must have met many a southern soldier who returned to his homeplace after the War to find it in shambles. By the War's end, the "cotton kingdom" of Mississippi and the rest of the South was gone, and if the fury of battle had not made the great plantation homes victims, the hard times and poor economy which followed did. *Windsor* was completed in 1861 in the last fleeting days before the War began, and—perhaps mercifully, considering what followed—its owner died shortly afterwards. The mansion was destroyed by fire in 1890.

Photographs by Regena H. Crutchfield

Vol. XIII   No. 3

Everybody's Magazine
The contents of this magazine are copyrighted and must not be reprinted without permission

Issued monthly. Yearly subscription, $1.00 in advance. Single copy, fifteen cents

Copyright, 1905, by The Ridgway-Thayer Company in the United States and Great Britain

Published by THE RIDGWAY-THAYER COMPANY, Union Square, New York City

ERMAN J. RIDGWAY, President   JOHN ADAMS THAYER, Secretary and Treasurer
10 Norfolk St., Strand, London, W. C. England

Everybody's Magazine. "The Natchez Trace," an article by John Swain which appeared in the highly popular *Everybody's Magazine* in September, 1905, is credited with drawing national attention to the history and romance of the old Natchez Trace. The author described part of the northern end of the Trace and illustrated his article with photographs made along the way.

Magazine courtesy of the Nashville Public Library

Union Bridge, which carried the Natchez Trace Road across the Harpeth River, south of Nashville, was one of the last covered bridges in Tennessee when it was destroyed by a flood in 1948. Built in 1881 on a section of the Natchez Trace which the United States Army had improved in the early 1800s, the bridge replaced an earlier one which had burned during the War Between the States. By then, of course, the Natchez Trace had long since lost its importance, and this section of its route was just another part of the county road system.

Photograph courtesy of the United States National Park Service

Swain Photo of Lewis Grave. The monument over the grave of Meriwether Lewis, dedicated by the State of Tennessee in 1848, had fallen into disrepair by 1905 when John Swain made his photographic journey along the Natchez Trace. Forest cover still dominated the site, which today is located in an immaculately mowed clearing on the Natchez Trace near Hohenwald, Tennessee.

Photograph from *Everybody's Magazine* courtesy of the Nashville Public Library

Napier Iron Furnace. The Napier iron industry was still going strong in the 1920s when this photo of its more modern furnace equipment was taken. By then, however, the mines were running out of the once-rich ore which had supported the smelters for close to one hundred years. In a short time, the furnaces would shut down forever.

Photograph from Bulletin 39 of the Tennessee Division of Geology

County Highway. The iron industry had its own railroad system to locally transport the iron from its smelters and the raw materials required for its making. After the closing of the furnaces, the railroad was of no further value, and so the tracks were pulled and the road bed was converted to a county highway.

Photograph courtesy of the United States National Park Service

Leiper's Fork Marker. The Daughters of the American Revolution and the Daughters of the War of 1812 were responsible for a clearer understanding of the original route of the Natchez Trace. Beginning early in the twentieth century, the Daughters of the American Revolution began marking the route with monuments. Over the next several years, the two organizations essentially completed their task. This marker, placed by the Daughters of the War of 1812, is located about a mile south of Leiper's Fork, Tennessee.

Photograph courtesy of the United States National Park Service

The Old Trace. This picture, taken along the old Natchez Trace during the 1930s, expresses better than a thousand words the peaceful environment associated with the Trace in the days immediately before the construction of the Natchez Trace Parkway. Representing just the opposite of the period when the Trace was one of the most traveled highways in the United States, this scene, like the Trace itself and the plantation economy which followed, has "gone with the wind."

Photograph courtesy of the United States National Park Service

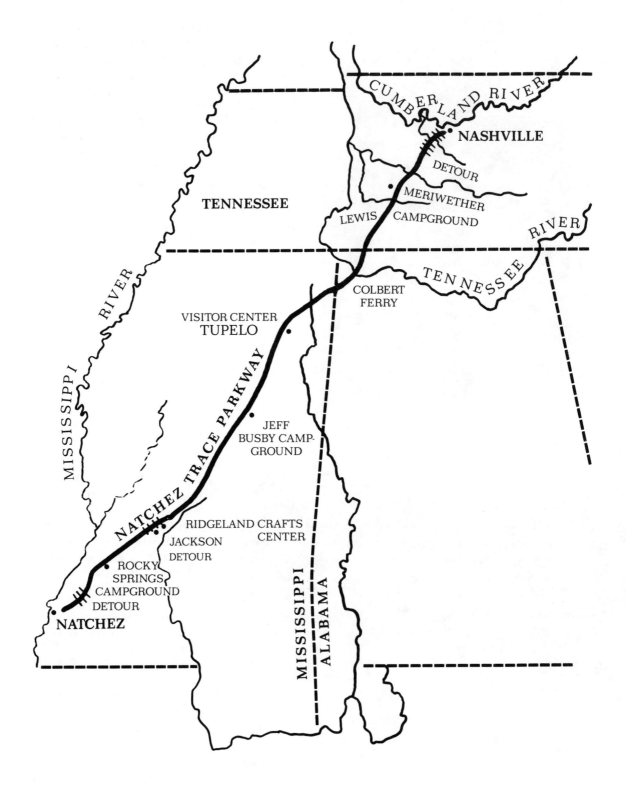

CHAPTER NINE

The Natchez Trace Parkway

It was not only the renewal of public interest in the Natchez Trace that was responsible for its salvation through the establishment of the Natchez Trace Parkway. The Great Depression and its accompanying woes wore heavily upon the minds of all Americans, and the rural people of Mississippi seemed to have had a particularly hard time making the best out of the situation. Overworked farms—"cotton poverty," as one historian has called it—were common all over the state, and much of the once fine land that had supported countless Indians and not a few proud plantations now lay in deep erosion. To Mississippians, it seemed a short time between Reconstruction and the poverty of the early twentieth century and the Depression.

Mississippi Congressman Thomas Jefferson Busby, a native of Tishomingo County, astride the Natchez Trace, perceived that a public works project which could catch the imagination and interest of the people could also be the salvation of the region in which it was situated by putting large numbers of unemployed people back to work for a prolonged period of time—or, at least until something better came along.

The Natchez Trace Parkway, except for three major sections, is complete between Nashville and Natchez. The Parkway passes through the states of Tennessee, Alabama, and Mississippi on its journey from the Cumberland River in the north to the Mississippi River in the south. While generally following the route of the old Natchez Trace, the Parkway does deviate from time to time because of right-of-way or other property rights considerations. For 450 miles the Parkway plunges through varied habitats, each displaying a unique form of plant cover and wildlife. The United States National Park Service has done a tremendous job in marking the Parkway and pointing out interesting natural, archaeological, and historical features. When completed, the Natchez Trace Parkway will provide the motorist with an uninterrupted journey which bridges the gap between time past and the twentieth century.

Drawing by James A. Crutchfield and Edison Travelstead

Busby thus introduced a resolution to Congress which called for an initial survey of the Natchez Trace. It is reported that the Department of the Interior took a dim view of the project, and that officially it urged President Roosevelt to veto the bill if it passed. It did pass Congress and FDR signed it into law, partially out of his need for the support of Mississippi Senator Pat Harrison, who sat on the powerful Senate Finance Committee and was in a position to help or harm Roosevelt's personal projects.

On May 21, 1934, an act was approved by the second session of the Seventy-Third Congress of the United States calling for "an appropriation of $50,000 with which to make a survey of the Old Indian Trail known as the 'Natchez Trace,' with a view of constructing a national road on the route to be known as the 'Natchez Trace Parkway.'" Citing that "the Natchez Trace was one of the most ancient and important Indian roads leading from the territory in the section of Tennessee about Nashville . . . through the Chickasaw and Choctaw Indian lands in what is now Mississippi . . . to Natchez," the act ear-marked the money for the purpose of surveying the Trace along its entire length as near to its original route as possible. From this survey, estimates for the actual construction of the proposed parkway would then be determined.

The National Park Service of the Department of the Interior received the $50,000 and in turn allocated $40,000 of the sum to the Bureau of Public Roads for performing the engineering survey and estimating the proposed parkway's cost. The remaining $10,000 was to be used by the Park Service itself to research the Trace's history and to design the master plan for the parkway's construction.

By 1935, the original survey as called for by the Congressional resolution was completed, and late in the same year a sum of $1,286,686 was consigned by the government for the initial phases of construction in Mississippi. Contracts for the first three road grading projects were let in 1937, following the acquisition of rights-of-way. Another $1,500,000 was allocated for fiscal year 1938, this amount being divided among the three states of Mississippi, Alabama, and Tennessee, based on the mileage of proposed parkway to be included in each state.

Finally, on May 18, 1938, the Natchez Trace Parkway was designated by the United States Congress to be an official unit in the National Park Service's system. During the next three years, from 1939 to 1941, funds totaling $3,550,000 were distributed for the Parkway's construction.

In 1941, Senate Document Number 148, entitled *Natchez Trace Parkway Survey*, was published by the U.S. Government Printing Office. Carrying the formidable sub-title, *Letter of the Secretary of the Interior Transmitting in Response to Senate Resolution 222, a Report of a Survey of the Old Indian Trail, Known as the Natchez Trace, Made by the Department of the Interior, Through the National Park Service, Pursuant to an Act Approved May 21, 1934 With a View to Constructing a National Road on the Route to be Known as the Natchez Trace Parkway,* the 167 page book set out in detail the history of the Trace from its earliest known times down to its demise at the beginning of the steamboat era. This comprehensive manual also contained the Department of the Interior's recommendations for the archaeological and historical sites along the Trace, as well as its plans for the future implementation of the Parkway.

From those early days of the Parkway's construction to today, through good times and bad, much of the construction along its proposed 450 mile route between Nashville and Natchez has been finished. However, there are three major sections—between Natchez and Port Gibson, around the Jackson area, and the last approximately twenty miles leading into Nashville—which lack completion. With national economic affairs as they are at this writing, there can be no sure timetable projected for the *total* completion of the project.

Today, the Natchez Trace Parkway is one of over 330 units in the system of national parks and monuments supervised by the United States National Park Service. Presently containing over 45,000 acres, the Parkway, as its *historian emeritus*, Dawson Phelps, has declared, "is not a highway, but a long narrow park." And so it is. In one place it might be no wider than the highway and a few feet of right-of-way on either side. Somewhere else, the property line might wander off into the woods for several hundred yards.

While thus far planned and implemented with an eye toward the history of the Natchez Trace, the National Park Service did not forget to include recreational aspects in the Parkway's design. Studded along its entire length are rest rooms, campgrounds, and picnic areas, and easy access to nearby towns provide today's traveler with a variety of overnight accommodations and restaurants. Swimming, boating, and fishing are permitted sports in selected locations. Attractive historical exhibits highlight the tourist's journey, and by merely stopping to read them one can obtain a very definitive history of the Natchez Trace and its place in the development of the young United States. Commercial transportation is prohibited, and so motorists can drive leisurely, enjoying the beauty of the countryside, unobstructed by billboards and highway signs.

There obviously are decided differences between the Natchez Trace of yesterday and the Natchez Trace Parkway of today. Yet the two are still akin. The old Trace died many years ago after a brief life as one of the Nation's most traveled highways. Today, it is reborn in the Natchez Trace Parkway, one of the most popular—and most visited—units in the National Park Service system.

Land Erosion. By the time Reconstruction was over and the twentieth century had begun, the once prosperous plantation economy of Mississippi and the rest of the old South was long forgotten. While the "cotton kingdom" was the essence of the ante-bellum South, its heavy demands on the soil left only an impoverished landscape as its lasting reward. In the early days of the twentieth century, "cotton poverty"—as the bibliographer, Thomas D. Clark, called it—had all but ruined hundreds of thousands of acres of southern farmland. Roads in which "every mudhole, rutted hillside, and rickety bridge had to be negotiated according to its own peculiar bit of treachery," in the words of Clark, typified the remains of the Natchez Trace, and the time was ripe for a

renaissance of the entire region. This eroded land, shown as it appeared in 1935, is located near Port Gibson in Claiborne County, Mississippi.

Photograph courtesy of the United States National Park Service

The Natchez Trace Parkway Survey, published in 1941, was the "Bible" for the later implementation and improvements along the Natchez Trace Parkway. Published as Senate Document Number 148 of the third session of the Seventy-Sixth Congress, the book is presently a scarce volume and commands a handsome price on the rare book market.

Book courtesy of the Nashville Public Library

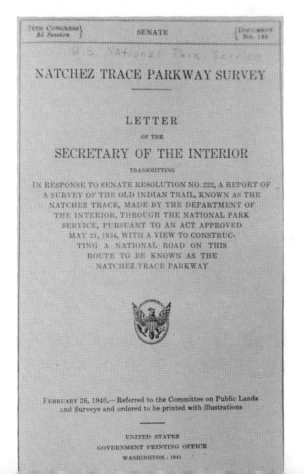

Emerald Mound Site. When Emerald Mound—originally called the Selsertown Site— was excavated by National Park Service archaeologists during the early days of the Parkway's development, it appeared as it does in this photograph. The site was described in the *Natchez Trace Parkway Survey* as lying "only about three-quarters of a mile from the Natchez Trace Parkway itself. This group at present contains only two mounds, situated upon a natural rectangular plateau-like elevation. . . .

Cultivation of these mounds has damaged them to some extent, and has softened the originally sharp outlines of the larger mound on the west." Compare this photo with the one on page 39 showing the same mound after restoration.

Photograph courtesy of the United States National Park Service

Bynum Mounds Dig. As soon as the Natchez Trace Parkway was approved, teams of National Park Service archaeologists moved into the area and systematically began to excavate and to interpret the prehistory of the region. The Bynum Mounds, located just south of Tupelo, were opened in the early 1940s, and a typical day at the dig site looked like the scene in this photo. It is only through the thorough, methodical, patient research of these dedicated public servants that we possess accurate knowledge today of the customs and lifestyles of the Prehistoric population along the Natchez Trace.

Photograph courtesy of the United States National Park Service

Mississippi CCC Camp. One of President Franklin Roosevelt's first public service acts was the establishment of the "CCC Boys," the Civilian Conservation Corps. Working on public lands all over the United States, the CCC was responsible for the creation and maintenance of thousands of miles of trails throughout the National Park system, as well as for the establishment of most of the picnic areas and camp sites in these parks. This photo shows the main "street" of a CCC Camp along the Mississippi portion of the Natchez Trace Parkway in the early 1940s.

Photograph courtesy of the United States National Park Service

Parkway Overpass. The Natchez Trace Parkway was designed to provide uninterrupted motorist travel from Nashville to Natchez. While country roads intersected the Parkway here and there, in many cases they were routed over or under the thoroughfare instead. This photo shows one of the first overpasses completed by the National Park Service on the Parkway.

Photograph courtesy of the United States National Park Service

The Blizzard of 1951 that visited much of the south brought record depths of snow and low temperatures throughout the region, and it was no stranger to the Natchez Trace Parkway. Several days of freezing rain, accompanied by sub-freezing and even sub-zero temperatures, provided scenes such as this one along the Parkway. Visualize the situation if one were traveling on foot in this type of weather and the next "civilized" place where one could get warm and obtain a half-decent meal and a night's lodging was still scores of miles away!

Photograph courtesy of the United States National Park Service

Barge on the Tennessee River. One of the most difficult obstacles in the construction of the Natchez Trace Parkway—just like it was the most difficult obstacle to the "Kaintucks" in their travels up the old Trace—was the crossing of the Tennessee River. Already swollen by the backwaters from Pickwick Dam, the river was much wider when the Parkway came along than it was in the early days of Natchez Trace travel. Nevertheless, with the help of barges such as this one, the river was bridged, and today's motorist along the Parkway travels easily over the river, whereas his early counterpart had to tolerate a time-consuming, and costly, ferry ride.

Photograph courtesy of the United States National Park Service

Jeff Busby Park. A fitting memorial to the "father" of the Natchez Trace Parkway is the Jeff Busby picnic area, located between Kosciusko and Tupelo. Dedicated on November 7, 1965, with the attendance of Busby's two grandsons, the area provides a nature trail, campground, service station, store, and restrooms. The nearby overlook is situated atop one of the highest points (603 feet) in the entire state of Mississippi.

Photograph courtesy of the United States National Park Service

Parkway Plane Crash. Consider what the "Kaintucks" would have thought had they come upon this scene in their travels up the old Natchez Trace. Having no place else to go, the pilot of this crippled airplane picked the seclusion of the Natchez Trace Parkway to crash-land his craft in 1965.

Photograph courtesy of the United States National Park Service

Natural Habitat of the Beaver.
When designing and imple-
menting the Natchez Trace
Parkway, the National Park
Service attempted, whenever
possible, to preserve the natural habitats which have existed
in the region since the beginning of time. The beaver was
originally native to the entire
three-state region of the
Natchez Trace. While at one
time trapped almost into extinction, it has made a dramatic comeback in recent
years throughout its original
range.

Photograph courtesy of the United States National
Park Service

Rustic Fence. Split rail and
snake rail fences seem to go
hand in hand with the frontier,
and along the Natchez Trace
Parkway these testimonials to
the ingenuity of America's
early settlers have been preserved or restored wherever
possible. As late as 1883, it was
estimated that there were over
six million miles of wood fence
in the United States, with a
value of over two billion dollars! Certainly, this variety of
fence had a prominent place in
the history of the region serviced by the Natchez Trace from
pioneer times on into the "plantation" era. The sight of these
examples today makes one ap-
preciate   the   simple—yet
efficient—technology of our
ancestors.

Photograph courtesy of the United States National
Park Service.

The Old Trace. The National Park Service has been careful to document the story of the old Natchez Trace all along its course, and whenever it is appropriate a roadside exhibit is displayed which enlightens the motorist to the pertinent facts about a particular area or subject. This exhibit, situated at the southern end of the Parkway, near Natchez, tells the whole story of the Trace in capsule form, thus setting the stage for the motorist to follow the history of the thoroughfare from one end to the other.

Photograph courtesy of the United States National Park Service

THE OLD TRACE

The Trace quickly became an important highway and mail route which made communication between Natchez and Washington, D.C., fairly safe and rapid.

Swift Postriders could carry the mail between Nashville and Natchez in less than 10 days.

Troops marched over the Trace in 1803 when war seemed near, and again in 1812 at the outbreak of war with Great Britain.

Ohio Valley pioneers floated their products to Natchez or New Orleans in flatboats and returned home afoot or on horseback over the Trace.

After 1820 steamboats carried most Natchez traffic. Parts of the Trace were then abandoned, other parts used as local roads.

Period Costumes. Today's National Park Service personnel portray the history of the region in a way that is unforgettable. Donning the attire of yesteryear, the staff participates in such activities as cooking over an open fire, as was the custom at many of the old stands along the Trace (right), and posing as a "Kaintuck" on his way up the Trace from Natchez to Nashville (left).

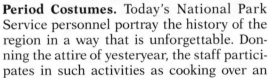
Photographs courtesy of the United States National Park Service

Water Skiing. Imagine the shock of the weary eighteenth or nineteenth century traveler upon the Natchez Trace if he were to approach Colbert's Ferry and see this scene! While not a favorite of the "Kaintucks" and post riders, water skiing does have a popular following at today's Colbert Ferry on the Tennessee River not far from the point where the original Natchez Trace crossed the waterway.

Photograph courtesy of the United States National Park Service

Parkway Recreational Facilities. Many recreational pursuits are available to the modern traveler along the Natchez Trace Parkway. Among the more popular ones are camping at either the Rocky Springs, Jeff Busby, or Meriwether Lewis campgrounds, cycling along any part of the Parkway's several hundred mile length, and horseback riding.

Photographs courtesy of the United States National Park Service

Meriwether Lewis Museum. This log museum, located near Hohenwald, Tennessee, houses material relevant to the Meriwether Lewis tragedy. The building is situated close to the site of Grinder's Stand, where Lewis mysteriously lost his life in 1809. Originally designated as part of the Meriwether Lewis National Monument, the structure and all of the monument acreage were eventually incorporated into the Natchez Trace Parkway system.

Photograph by Regena H. Crutchfield

Mount Locust, one of the earliest stands on the old Natchez Trace, has been restored by the National Park Service, and appears to the modern visitor much as it did in the days when it provided overnight accommodations for weary travelers along the Trace. Located north of Natchez, Mount Locust probably was built as early as 1780 as a one-room cabin. Completely furnished with examples of "inn" furniture and utensils, Mount Locust conjures up the image of the past and lets one's imagination slip easily into yesteryear. The National Park Service maintains a "living history" program at this location, and its personnel portray life styles as they were along the Natchez Trace during its heyday.

Photograph by Regena H. Crutchfield

The Ridgeland Crafts Center, located on the Parkway north of Jackson, features exhibits and demonstrations of Mississippi crafts. Built by the National Park Service to popularize the arts and handicrafts of the region, the Center attracts thousands of visitors annually.

Photograph courtesy of the United States National Park Service

The Gordon House, home of John Gordon, the operator of Gordon's Ferry across the Duck River, still stands, and the National Park Service is hopeful of converting it into a visitor center when the northern section of the Parkway is complete. The house has been steadily occupied until recently, when government possession was obtained. In olden times, when a traveler crossed Gordon's Ferry he knew that it was only a "whoop and a holler" to Nashville.

Photograph courtesy of the United States National Park Service

Near Colbert's Ferry. The original Natchez Trace probably looked much like this remnant near Colbert's Ferry. In all cases where possible, the National Park Service has left sections of the old Trace just as they were when traveled by the "Kaintucks" and the post riders.

Photograph courtesy of the United States National Park Service

Bay Springs Lock. The engineering miracle of the twentieth century may be the Tennessee–Tombigbee Canal. Linking the inland Tennessee River with the Gulf of Mexico via the Tombigbee and Alabama rivers, the "Tenn-Tom" eliminates hundreds of miles of travel—as well as millions of dollars of costs—for many industrial and commercial sections of the South. One of the combination locks and dams on the "Tenn-Tom" is at Bay Springs, located just off the Natchez Trace in Mississippi. Here, within a few hundred yards of each other, are one of the most sophisticated roads

of the early nineteenth century and the ultimate waterway of the late twentieth century.
Drawing courtesy of the United States Army Corps of Engineers

Scenic Beauty along the Parkway. This typical scene along the Natchez Trace demonstrates very effectively the beauty of today's Parkway. Weaving through hundreds of miles of hills, lowlands, forests, and swamps, the Parkway cuts through a cross-section of southern Americana—natural and manmade—at its best.
Photograph couresty of the United States National Park Service

Natchez Trace Marker. The arrowhead points the way to a segment of the old Natchez Trace as preserved along the route of the new Natchez Trace Parkway. Linking today and yesterday, the Parkway sheds more insight into the events of the early Southwest along its meticulously marked route than any other source of history.

Photograph courtesy of the United States National Park Service

Bibliography

Abernethy, Thomas Perkins: *The Burr Conspiracy*, Oxford University Press, New York, 1954.

Baily, Francis: *Journal of a Tour in Unsettled Parts of North America in 1796 & 1797*, Feffer and Simons, Inc., London, 1866; Southern Illinois University, Carbondale, Illinois, 1969.

Botkin, B. A., Editor: "John A. Murrell's Own Story" in *A Treasury of Southern Folklore*, Bonanza Books, New York, 1980.

Breazeale, J. W. M.: *Life As It Is*, Knoxville, 1842; Charles Elder, Nashville, 1969.

Burchard, Ernest F.: *The Brown Iron Ores of the Western Highland Rim, Tennessee*, Tennessee Department of Geology, Nashville, 1934.

Cantwell, Robert: *Alexander Wilson—Naturalist and Pioneer*, J. B. Lippincott Company, Philadelphia, 1961.

Coates, Robert M.: *The Outlaw Years*, The Literary Guild of America, New York, 1930.

Crutchfield, James A.: *Early Times in the Cumberland Valley*, First American National Bank, Nashville, 1976.

———: *The Harpeth River: A Biography*, Blue and Gray Press, Nashville, 1972.

———: *Williamson County—A Pictorial History*, The Donning Company, Virginia Beach, 1980.

Daniels, Jonathan: *The Devil's Backbone*, McGraw-Hill Book Company, New York, 1962.

Dodd, Donald B. and Dodd, Wynelle S.: *Historical Statistics of the South—1790–1970*, University of Alabama Press, University, Alabama, 1973.

Dunbar, Seymour: *A History of Travel in America*, Tudor Publishing Company, New York, 1937.

Eastern National Park and Monument Association: *Mount Locust on the Old Natchez Trace*, n.p., n.d.

Federal Writers' Project: *Mississippi: A Guide to the Magnolia State*, New York, 1938.

Folsom, Franklin: *America's Ancient Treasures*, Rand McNally & Company, New York, 1971.

Gabriel, Ralph Henry, Editor: *The Pageant of America*, 15 volumes, Yale University Press, New Haven, 1925–1929.

Guild, Jo. C.: *Old Times in Tennessee*, Nashville, 1878; Tenase, Knoxville, 1971.

James, Marquis: *The Life of Andrew Jackson*, The Bobbs-Merrill Company, Indianapolis, 1938.

Johnson, Leland R.: *Engineers on the Twin Rivers*, U.S. Army Corps of Engineers, Nashville, 1978.

McCracken, Harold: *George Catlin and the Old Frontier*, The Dial Press, New York, 1959.

Michaux, F. A.: *Travels to the Westward of the Allegany Mountains*, Richard Phillips, London, 1805.

Myer, William E.: *Indian Trails of the Southeast*, Washington, 1928; Blue and Gray Press, Nashville, 1971.

National Geographic Society: *Clues to America's Past*, Washington, 1976.

Phelps, Dawson A.: "The Natchez Trace—Indian Trail to Parkway" in the *Tennessee Historical Quarterly*, Nashville, September, 1962.

Rose, Albert C.: *Historic American Roads*, Crown Publishers, Inc., New York, 1976.

Royce, Charles C.: *Indian Land Cessions in the United States*, Bureau of American Ethnology, Washington, 1899.

Skates, John R.: *Mississippi—A History*, W. W. Norton & Company, New York, 1979.

Smith, J. Frazer: *White Pillars*, William Helburn, New York, 1941.

Swain, John: "The Natchez Trace" in *Everybody's Magazine*, New York, September, 1905.

Swanton, John R.: *Early History of the Creek Indians and their Neighbors*, Bureau of American Ethnology, Washington, 1922.

————: *Indian Tribes of the Lower Mississippi Valley and Adjacent Coast of the Gulf of Mexico*, Bureau of American Ethnology, Washington, 1911.

————: *The Indian Tribes of North America*, Bureau of American Ethnology, Washington, 1952.

————: *The Indians of the Southeastern United States*, Washington, 1946; Smithsonian Institution Press, Washington, 1979.

Terrell, John Upton: *American Indian Almanac*, The World Publishing Company, New York, 1971.

Tunis, Edwin: *Frontier Living*, The World Publishing Company, Cleveland, 1961.

United States Government Printing Office: *Natchez Trace Parkway Survey*, Washington, 1941.

Ward, Ralph T.: *Steamboats*, The Bobbs-Merrill Company, Indianapolis, 1973.

Wellman, Paul I.: *Spawn of Evil*, Doubleday and Company, New York, 1964.

Williams, Samuel Cole: *Adair's History of the American Indians*, The Watauga Press, Johnson City, Tennessee, 1930.

Wilson, Josleen: *The Passionate Amateur's Guide to Archaeology in the United States*, Collier Books, New York, 1980.

Wright, Jr., J. Leitch: *The Only Land They Knew*, The Free Press, New York, 1981.

Index